Grace

Grace

---

freeing
the swan within
for a beautiful life

NANCY MAIR

Daybreak™ Books
An Imprint of Rodale Books
New York, New York

Copyright © 1998 by Nancy Mair

Daybreak is a trademark of Rodale Press, Inc.

Printed in the United States of America

Cover Designer: Jane Colby Knutila
Cover Illustrator: Steven Bender
Interior Designer: Faith Hague

Library of Congress Cataloging-in-Publication Data
Mair, Nancy,
    Grace : freeing the swan within for a beautiful life / Nancy Mair.
        p.   cm.
    ISBN 0–87596–504–0 hardcover
    1. Grace (Aesthetics).   I. Title.
    BH301.G7M35   1998
    179'.9—dc21   97–35053

Distributed in the book trade by St. Martin's Press

2 4 6 8 10 9 7 5 3 1 hardcover

┌──────── OUR PURPOSE ────────┐

*"We publish books that empower
people's minds and spirits."*

~

Dedicated to J. Donald Walters, from whom I have received years of priceless guidance, boundless insights, deep inspiration, and unfathomable friendship.

Contents

Acknowledgments

My deep appreciation goes always to Ginger deLeeuw, whose friendship knows no bounds; Cathy Parojinog for her unfailing support and late nights and weekends proofreading; Ali Patricia McKeon, who shared, along with her friendship, her knowledge on using colors and clothing to bring harmony between the inner self and outward expression; Alan Heubert for his years of encouragement; Jyotish Novak; Joseph and Anandi Cornell; Uma Macfarlane; Sue Loper-Powers, R.N., M.N., Women's Health nurse practitioner and clinical ayurvedic specialist, for her vast medical and holistic health knowledge; Sara Cryer, who got me started on the right track; Adam and Nila Borstein of Ananda Yoga for Self-Awareness; Virginia Cayer and Erika Scheckells of V.J.'s Good Reviews; and the many friends whose stories and inspirations fill these pages.

I have the warmest regard and appreciation for Sheree Bykofsky, my literary agent and friend, for her inspiration behind this book and for following her intuition against all reason; and for Karen Kelly, a gracious and superb editor.

Most of all, my boundless gratitude goes to my husband, Kerry, for his deep faith in me—and for his great patience and love that enabled him to spend many months being married more to a book than to a wife.

CHAPTER 1

~

Grace: The Universal Flow of Energy

s a teenager, I always knew that I had pushed things too far when my father brought up the topic of sending me off to the nearby boarding school that specialized in instructing young women in social skills and graces. He always hoped that I would awaken to the delights of becoming an obedient, dutiful daughter. Finishing school held much more allure for him than it did for me. I saw it as his gravest threat. I would let him know, with my customary charm, that I wouldn't stay at such an awful place if he sent me there—and I also immediately improved my grades and behavior.

For a woman, blind obedience to one's husband or parents was once the reigning edict behind grace. In the Victorian age, gracefulness through movement, speech, and social behavior was clearly cataloged—and essential for a woman's social acceptance. The basic rules of behavior were taught to women at an early age, and strict observance was enforced by their husbands and parents. Things were done a certain way, and that was that. Exceptions were few.

In the late 1800s, the model woman in London society would not consider it proper behavior to read newspapers, show interest in political matters, engage in intellectual pursuits, or voice an opinion contrary to her husband's views. A woman was to concern herself with sewing and mending, cleaning, managing the household, keeping the children well-mannered and out of the way, and tending to the complete comfort of her husband. Ideally, she would have a slender waist; be graceful, charming, and pretty; and show a knack for light conversation and a gift for entertaining. She was to adore her husband worshipfully—or at least act as though she did. Of course, a woman in upper society could also arrange flowers; paint lovely pictures; do embroidery, lacework, and needlepoint; help the less fortunate; and make or receive afternoon social calls for a little variety.

Any woman who veered from the social norm became an immediate outcast and would never again be accepted by "normal" society. Her friends were obligated to shun her.

Divorce in those days was practically unthinkable. The husband owned his wife, the children, and all property and income—even if the possessions had been inherited by the woman. If she left the marriage, she became penniless, homeless, and had no rights to ever see her children again. She owned nothing—not even the clothes on her back. Naturally, she lost her social standing along with all her belongings. Her women-friends were forced to turn away because they didn't have any means to help and were compelled to obey the men of their houses.

This repression of women and anyone in a "lower class" was considered totally acceptable but silently devastated the people this attitude affected.

With great enthusiasm, the stifling strictures of the past have been banished with the unfolding of the twentieth century. But we have little direction in this new era. What is acceptable, and what is not? What is grace? Is grace even something that we want? Is it possible for everyone to express it? Isn't there something more vital than a person's ability to follow social customs and move in a graceful manner?

> True grace is timeless and resides within each one of us. It reaches levels far deeper than mere superficial display.
>
> ~

The meaning of grace is confusing to both women and men in our present era. The social rebellion against the old, restrictive standards of behavior has reached a point where people are ready to look deeper for the real essence of grace.

True grace is timeless and resides within each one of us. It reaches levels far deeper than mere superficial display. It involves more than social or physical form and is expressed in many ways, according to one's temperament—beauty through fluidity of thought, movement, and creative expression; an attitude of cooperation and respect for others; sincerity; a feeling of balance and harmony; love. It is a unique experience for each individual—something that was not taken into account in ages past.

A ballet performed with exquisite grace and beauty is inspiring and uplifting to behold. The effect would be shattered, however, if the audience were to see the dancers coming off the stage only to shout at one another, stand with poses of arrogance, and make crude remarks. True beauty of dance incorporates a harmony of spirit along with a harmony of action.

A person who is physically unable to be graceful in his movements can emanate a gracefulness of thought, form, and spirit that goes deeper than the physical realm. In our present times, who a person is is just starting to become more important than what a person looks like or what he can do. Concern for others, an expansive and optimistic outlook, and considerate words more than compensate for any physical inability.

Grace, when expressed through one's attitude toward other people and toward life, is reflected in the presence of graciousness. Graciousness is the outward social form of grace that shows sincere respect and courtesy to others under all circumstances. It requires as much skill and finesse as any physical achievement. And further, it lends an inner, radiant beauty to the person who can attain this inspiring attribute.

Grace is a form of consciousness. It is a universal energy available to everyone. To be able to experience the flow of grace in our lives requires being conscious of our actions and attitudes. It is being aware of the effect we have on others. The more sensitive we become to the consequences of our behavior, the more we can attune ourselves to grace.

~

The Experience of Grace

Grace is like the very air we breathe. We can't see the air that surrounds us, but we know it is there. Grace envelops us all. It can be brought to bear far more often than the occasional glimpses most people settle for. Through conscious appreciation of its benefits, grace can be brought into daily life.

When anyone bemoans the fact that he can't feel the presence of grace, it isn't because grace has veered away and gone elsewhere. People have mood swings and may change directions on a whim. Grace does not. We nearly all get sidetracked by the events in our lives from time to time and forget about, or ignore, the existence of grace. That's all it is; we turn away from grace and then no longer see it. Once we reconnect with it, we see that it never went away. It is up to us to make the connection with this positive, expansive, life-affirming energy. No one else can do it for us.

Grace can be experienced in a vast number of ways. We connect with grace through spiritual beliefs, communing with spirit in nature, bringing inspiration to other people, or improving our lives, our society, or the world at large. Grace is a *living* presence. It throbs with inspiration and new ideas, small miracles of life, and expansive and unifying beliefs.

Grace is applied in our daily lives through our thoughts and actions. Each time we think or act in an uplifting, inspiring, or positive way, we attune ourselves to the consciousness of grace. This consciousness, in turn, becomes more and more a part of our lives, a part of who we are and who we become. Then, too, when we become vehicles for inspiring or uplifting others, we are uplifted as well.

Everyone wants to experience some element of inner peace, deep contentment, and more harmony. These are states that are *attained*; they are not merely passive lulls in the turmoil of life's ups and downs. They are realized through personal victory in overcoming trials or difficulties and by learning from life's lessons. These inner qualities cannot be gained by avoiding all conflict or hiding in a protective shelter. Hiding from life brings an inner emptiness; it doesn't bring peace, contentment, or inner harmony. These sublime qualities are aspects of grace that can permeate one's whole being until, at last, one's entire consciousness vibrates with the inner balm of awareness and understanding. As we build and maintain a harmonious balance between our thoughts and actions, we live more freely in the uplifting reality of grace.

Expressions of Grace

In its exalted form, grace in movement and thought links us to the Supreme Spirit. Our consciousness is uplifted until we become an embodiment of love, inspiration, peace, wisdom, or courage. We are filled with reverence for all life and devotion to higher ideals. Our highest self radiates outward from the core of our being in waves of deepest joy.

Grace is an inner beauty, which grows and emerges in greater loveliness, like the swan in *The Ugly Duckling* whose beauty was hidden in its unenlightened youth but unfolded into full radiance when it matured.

The image of the swan is used in more than children's fairy tales. The graceful beauty of the swan is represented in Eastern scriptural lore as the vehicle for the Supreme Spirit. This spirit, which flows into and through all life, rides on the wings of grace.

Grace is essential for our lasting happiness, success, and prosperity. It will manifest in our lives corresponding to our specific nature. Each one of us is a unique expression of life. Though we have our similarities and our common link through humanity, no two individuals are exactly alike in the way they look, think, and act. We are each significant in our own ways.

There are as infinite a number of pathways to grace as there are individuals. We can find and express grace through motherhood, relationships, business or a career, the sciences, the arts, sports, music, dance, or an attunement to nature. All of these are creative expressions of grace when they are based on harmony, truth, and beauty of design or spirit.

The classic social gestures of grace are naturally included—those of entertaining, where friends, family, and acquaintances are honored through a spirit of goodwill and appreciation, and in cooking for others and serving them, which nurtures and nourishes through a loving exchange of energy. Grace also encompasses loveliness in our surroundings. A beautiful home and garden depict a restful haven. And presenting ourselves attractively, with good posture, neatness, and a pleasing use of color, indicates to others our innate sensitivity, dignity, and self-respect. Additionally, greeting everyone graciously embraces beauty through our words and tone of voice.

Grace also resides in the noble fight for an improved society and in the quest for higher ideals.

The art of diplomacy, be it between nations, in business, in the workplace, or at home, is an admirable form of grace. Bringing two differing views into agreement or resolution is ennobling to all involved when it is based on a true desire to see that the best, most honorable solution for everyone is reached.

Good manners were the basis for grace in the old tradition, and they are sadly lacking in today's era of vying to get what we deserve or what is rightfully ours. Those who always put themselves first will find that they end up getting little in return. It is a contractive energy that yields less and less as it turns in upon itself. The lack of satisfaction that comes from caring only about oneself can lead to a rude and resentful temperament. It is not enjoyable for the individual whose thoughts are swarming with discontent, nor is it pleasant for one's colleagues and friends.

Consideration for others helps us to reflect more kindly upon our own faults and imperfections. If we can accept or

forgive something in another, we are more able to treat ourselves with the same regard. Conversely, if we don't mentally
object when we treat others in a less-than-thoughtful way, it
hardly seems fair to resent similar treatment in turn.

Why Do We Want Grace?

An expansive outlook is accompanied by an inner sense
of fulfillment. A contractive, self-absorbed consciousness is accompanied by misery and bitterness.

There is much emphasis nowadays on opening the heart,
getting in tune with how we feel, feeling the heart's love,
bonding, learning to love and accept ourselves, and many
more examples of a society seeking growth, improvement, and
an expanded awareness of the potentials that lie within us.

There is also a growing perception throughout the world
of how our actions impact our environment and the people of
the world. Our vision and understanding of life is expanding.

The ecology movement has made the general public conscious of a need to preserve what we have and to restore what
is depleted. Much of the world has awakened from the cava-
lier attitude that allowed us, heedlessly, to take whatever we
wanted from the Earth and its waters for the sake of personal
profit or technological progress. We have seen the results of
this increased awareness in the widespread implementation of
recycling programs that are sponsored by cities and towns
across the country. Children's educational programs even focus

on a need to recycle and on ways to be more thoughtful about the products we use and their eventual disposal.

On a humanistic level, people are seeking ways to spread peace on Earth and find serenity in their own lives. An individual act of goodwill reverberates out into society as that person kindheartedly touched is inspired to likewise spread kindness to another. Maybe you have seen the bumper stickers "Practice random acts of kindness and senseless acts of beauty," or been the recipient of this sentiment. Recently, a friend of mine was driving in rush-hour traffic through a large metropolis. When she reached a tollbooth, she was told that the driver of the car in front of her had paid her way. She had no idea who the person was and was warmly affected by the unexpected gesture. As more people act with grace and harmony, it can be carried forth to reach far-distant people and regions.

These directions are being enthusiastically embraced because they will improve our lives, our society, and the world we live in. These same principles are the foundation of grace. That which improves oneself, one's community, one's country, or the world is worthwhile, inspiring, and inwardly fulfilling.

Why do we want grace in our lives? Because our lives become empty and devoid of purpose unless we aspire to higher levels of awareness and understanding. The more areas where grace is expressed, the more it can permeate our entire way of life—though even one avenue, one quality of expression, is enough to open the channel for grace to flow into one's life abundantly.

- Grace is based on universal principles, not just social convention. It can be expressed in various ways, according to one's temperament: through fluidity of movement, creative expression, an attitude of cooperation and respect for others, sincerity, an awareness of the underlying balance and harmony in life, and through love.
- Grace is an inner beauty, attainable to everyone.
- Grace is based on an inward experience first; then it can flow freely into any area of one's life.
- Attunement to grace bestows an expansive, inspiring approach to life.
- Grace blends a harmony of spirit with a harmony of action.

CHAPTER 2

Redefining the Role
of Women

eminine grace in decades past was well-developed in its superficial form. It stifled and destroyed any true expression of grace because it was not based on a woman's personal reality but on social standards. How a woman truly felt was not a consideration at all. She was expected to behave in accordance with her parents', husband's, or family's rules. Well, good riddance to that. But where does independence of action lead?

It is definitely unpleasant to encounter what I think of as the "female bulldozer." In their enthusiasm for female independence, these bulldozers flatten all obstacles that dare to get in their way. Of course, it is important to be firm and strong, but that's not the same thing as destroying everything and everyone in the way.

Understandably, there is a strong desire for the freedom to choose our own paths through life—for women and men. In our society, the social norms of traditional roles are gradually dissolving, allowing mutual participation in all occupations. It is exciting to have so many opportunities, but this change has brought confusion. Does a woman need to act "tough like a man" to fill the male role or position? Is a man weakened when he is tender and loving or performs "women's work"?

Each individual is made up of aspects that were typically thought to be divided into manlike traits, oriented toward goals and results, and womanly characteristics of sensitivity, compassion, and service to others. But there is no quality that is exclusive to one gender. Women can be inwardly driven toward achievement, and men can be sensitive with a compassionate desire to serve the people of the world.

We all need to develop a balance between these differing male and female aspects within ourselves. But it is awkward in this era. We are exploring new territory and breaking down previous societal barriers for women and men. How to bring acceptance and harmony to the situation has been unclear.

In the midst of these upheavals, it's crucial for women and men to retain graciousness for the progress we have made to be accepted and integrated into our society at large.

Fear of Change

My sister and I were raised with the premise that when we grew up, we would marry, have children, and raise our families while leading correspondingly traditional lives in pleasant neighborhoods. Well, that was my parents' idea anyway. I had no reason to argue the concept. That was just the way it was. My sister, being older than I, showed the first signs of not cooperating with the agenda. I bided my time.

My father was always delighted that I loved to cook and enjoyed the domestic realm. He overlooked my strong, stubborn drive for achieving goals that I set for myself. To him, I showed all signs of being a nice, conventional wife.

After my mother passed on, I temporarily took over the social role and household management that had been my mother's fields of interest. I cooked for my father and accompanied him to the theater, symphonies, and the opera. I was often his companion when he dined with close friends. I would even journey with him to distant countries as his traveling companion. He occasionally remarked on an irrepressible streak in me, but he couldn't really complain.

Then, one day I saw a film that sparked an intense desire to fly in a balloon. I became very excited about ballooning and was obsessed with going for a flight. My father, when he heard the idea, said, "You're not flying in a balloon!" and left the room. Frankly, I saw no reason why I shouldn't and promptly wrote a letter to the only balloon company within three states and mailed it before my father could find out. (This was in the early years of hot-air ballooning, when balloons were quite rare.) My father didn't know that I planned to follow my yearning for adventure, as my sister had done before me.

I think that it still rankled my father a bit that my sister, after earning honors all through school, had departed for southeast Alaska, where she bought her own commercial fishing boat and was earning a living catching salmon. He didn't want to see this type of thing happen to *both* of his daughters. I was then 20 years old, and he hoped in vain that he could divert this new interest.

Several months later, I was joyously earning my commercial pilot's license for hot-air balloons—with my father's begrudging support. I was still preparing all his meals for him, and he may just have figured that it was best to humor me. But he didn't talk about my new ventures to any of his friends. I think he felt that he had made a big mistake somewhere in child-rearing to have produced two daughters who were not sticking with convention. He didn't seem to object to other women who sought to follow their own dictates. He just didn't like to see it in his own daughters.

I never considered myself a feminist because I didn't notice that there were things that women weren't supposed to do. I just did them. But I did notice that when I spent a long time striving hard for something or spent most of my time doing hard physical work, it affected my personality. I became more "masculine," more driving, less sensitive to other people's feelings, harder on myself and others. It wasn't exactly a good thing. I didn't know how to be assertive and achievement-oriented while at the same time retain the outwardly gentler qualities of kindness and sensitivity. There were no guidelines on how to be both.

I was fortunate to have a loyal friend, Sylvia, who let me

know when I started ordering people around too much. Sylvia was my appointed crew chief for the balloon flights in my newly founded balloon business. She was reliable and, equally important, a lot of fun to be with. The first time she directed a gentle rebuke in my direction was early one morning, just after sunrise. We were laying out the balloon in a dew-covered field, and I started in with a list of commands, telling my crew what I wanted them to do. Sylvia was justifiably annoyed and said, "You could at least ask nicely," as she walked off to do what I had asked. That gave me something to think about. Here my crew was getting up at 4:00 A.M. to help with my flight, and I wasn't even being considerate of them. How easy it is to take people for granted. I did my best to change. She had to tell me again on occasion, when I reverted to my goal-oriented let's-get-this-done attitude. I can claim that I was sometimes under a lot of stress, but that doesn't absolve the need for good manners, sincere thanks, and appreciation of others. I still guard against slipping into a commanding voice and attitude, especially when I'm overseeing a job or project. I have silently thanked Sylvia countless times over the years for her honesty and friendship during our years of working together.

A driving personality does not need to be reinforced by a commanding voice. It is better to balance forceful energy with increased awareness of others. Are we treating people with the same consideration that we would like extended to us? It can be difficult to maintain this perspective when a goal is in sight. It is also the best time to remember it.

~

Choices for Women

It's fascinating to me that there are some women who now feel embarrassed or inadequate because they are focusing on taking care of their children or family and not pursuing a career. That's a switch. It used to be that only women who chose a career over family were the ones who felt like social misfits. Now both categories feel that they should be doing more.

Says who? There is no single path that is correct for every woman. What matters most is that what you choose to do—be it having a family, a family and a career, or exclusively a career—brings out the best that is in you. There is no point in trying to force yourself into a role that doesn't suit your temperament. That's just what women are trying to break away from.

The Woman at Home

Some women thrive on managing a household. It takes an incredible amount of energy to raise children, create a nurturing home, and spend time seeing that the family is well taken care of. For many women, it is more fulfilling than any career. I have the greatest admiration for women whose focus and goals are centered on tending to the needs of their families.

Caring for and nurturing one's family is a great accomplishment, and one that the career-oriented woman may discover is more exhausting and frustrating than any challenges in the workplace. At least with a "job" it is possible to leave at the end of the day. Not so for the woman at home. The people and surroundings are always there for her to deal with as best as possible—24 hours a day—and usually she receives less recognition or appreciation than a person who works outside the home.

Even without children, running a household is quite a feat. The slot typically filled by children may alternatively be filled by friends. Adults as well as children enjoy a place where they are cared for and nurtured. If life at home is deeply satisfying, there is absolutely no need to give excuses for not doing more. All people need some place of refuge and someone to provide it.

Family and Career Woman

Many women not only wish to have children but also want to have outside interests and goals apart from child-rearing and family life. Incorporating these two lifestyles requires a real balancing act: determining when the family needs attention and preventing that from adversely affecting one's career. There is probably no way a woman can fully take care of a house, children, and husband plus devote lots of energy to a career. This doesn't mean that both can't be done, just that things need to be prioritized. What is most important to you and your family? A spotless house? Carefully prepared meals? Laundry folded and put away? Outings together? Time to relax together and enjoy one another's company?

The needs of others—children, spouse, partner, or roommate—ought to be taken into consideration when a woman splits her life between home and work. But those needs must be balanced with the deep yearning to find expression through both motherhood and career. The self-respect a woman feels when she honors herself and her own needs enables her to accept the limitations that come with managing two separate facets of life. Then her children, spouse, or other companions will feel that energy of respect and respond accordingly. Well, maybe not all of the time, but it will give them the opportunity to learn to respect another's choices, whatever they may be.

Unfortunately, a sense of guilt usually worms its way into our thoughts whenever we think that we should be doing more—even if it is impossible. Respecting whatever is being done both at home and at work and constantly reevaluating the priorities will do much to keep the two areas in balance. Acting with love, respect, and cooperation will demonstrate more than words can say. Doing one's best to provide a loving environment at home while also making a productive contribution at work is a worthwhile goal.

> **When it comes to the final evaluation of what is most important in one's life, it is crucial to remember that success for a woman is pretty empty when it excludes the happiness and presence of others.**

There are countless ways to achieve a satisfying balance. My sister, who now works as an attorney during 10 months of the year and then goes out on her fishing boat (with her husband) during salmon season, would much rather catch a fish than cook it. Fortunately, her husband loves to cook and is also quite willing to participate in caring for their children and running the household. But in each case there are always some compromises to be made.

When it comes to the final evaluation of what is most important in one's life, it is crucial to remember that success for a woman is pretty empty when it excludes the happiness and presence of others.

The Career Woman

The totally career-oriented woman, who may not have the desire to bear or raise children, finds her greatest personal fulfillment in pursuing work with all her energy. It is an outwardly satisfying life but still needs to be kept in balance by giving heartfelt energy to others. Doing this is awkward and sometimes quite difficult for women who find themselves emphasizing their mental or masculine qualities more than their sensitive feminine aspects. The career woman may feel little, if any, affinity with the domestic realm and may be more comfortable channeling her nurturing energy and supportive dedication into her job and the people associated with it.

Women who make the choice of having a profession rather than children are likely to find themselves having to make excuses for this presumed inadequacy. There are still some people who feel free to question a woman's choice in the matter. But it can hardly be considered a gracious act to have children for the sake of appearances when there is no interest in raising them from infancy to adulthood.

There are many avenues for expressing creative energy

other than through having children. To be successful in a career requires the same dedicated energy that family life requires. But for the career woman, the majority of her energy may be directed toward achieving goals outside the home. As with the woman who chooses family life and a career, there is the need to prioritize work with home life, but in this case the profession will usually take precedence. Yet everyone must have some kind of life outside the workplace.

I realize that I am more fortunate than many, in that my husband, Kerry, has never tried (or even cared) to get between me and my work. He has always encouraged, or been tolerant of, my various interests. I sometimes go through phases when I need to devote a great deal of extra time and energy to a job, but I then try to balance those times by refreshing our relationship and life at home.

I mostly work out of our house, which at least allows me to see Kerry, but it also means that our home is not always a sanctuary. Occasionally, I even have catering projects that require me to be in our kitchen from 6:00 A.M. until midnight. People file in and out of the house helping in various shifts, and mealtime can turn into a small party. When Kerry comes down for morning coffee, there may be several people chatting and working away. He never knows who, or how many, will be around. His "quiet" evenings after work reverberate with the clamor of mixers, blenders, juicers, and food processors, and the amplified voices trying to be heard above all the racket. This cannot be a restful time for Kerry, but he has never complained. He makes the best of it and usually joins in the activity.

As soon as the project is over, I make sure that we have some fun, relaxing evenings together. I make meals for Kerry that I know he will love, with special touches to show how deeply I appreciate him. Even if it is a quick, simple dinner, I add fresh herbs to the salad and put candles on the table. If I'm willing to give my time and energy to others, I need to give both to him as well.

I usually use food to express my love, as cooking comes most naturally to me, but I vary it a bit to keep the tokens unexpected. I might bring in loads of firewood for the woodstove in the winter months, clean up the garage or toolshed, or do some other chore that Kerry would normally handle.

I work with the larger rhythms of time, not only the day-to-day events. I can't always balance our life together from one day to the next but can manage to do so in the long run.

Personally, I require time with my husband and friends and a welcoming home to feel my best, but the degree of interest in home life differs widely among working women. Find your own way to balance the goal-oriented vision of a career with the nurturing qualities of the heart to bring graciousness into your life.

Balancing Feminine and Masculine Energies

Each person has feminine and masculine characteristics to his personality. These characteristics can be roughly classified as "qualities of the heart" for feminine attributes and "qualities of the mind" for masculine attributes. These are universal inclinations that are manifest to a greater or lesser degree in all people.

A list of feminine virtues includes compassion, receptivity, kindness, forgiveness, tenderness, servicefulness, love, adaptability, and cooperation with other people.

Two primary masculine virtues are direction, or goal-orientation, and a broad, impersonal view (compared to the feminine inclination to be personal with views or opinions). Added to this are an analytical mind, discrimination, being convinced of the rightness of one's ideas, concentration, a competitive spirit, and mental alertness.

Obviously, both men and women can have equal helpings of feminine and masculine qualities. Women who are recognized as being exceptional people often display such masculine traits as an analytical mind, discrimination, or a competitive spirit.

Jackie Joyner-Kersee is a phenomenal athlete, who combines a strong drive for achievement with a competitive spirit, discrimination applied to training and tactics in competition, focused concentration, the conviction that what she is undertaking is the correct thing to do, and mental alertness for knowing when to apply herself to her fullest. She also balances her achievements with a strength of femininity through servicefulness in developing the growth of track-and-field sports among children; kindness, consideration, and cooperation with other people; and a receptivity that allows her to listen to the advice and opinions of others in her career and personal life. She has flooded energy into both her masculine and feminine elements to grow in harmony with her inner nature.

Similarly, truly great men incorporate into their personalities the feminine attributes of compassion, service to others, and kindness. The strength of purpose and driving force associated with men is enhanced by these feminine qualities.

The Nobel laureate Albert Schweitzer (1875–1965), who is probably best known for his missionary hospital work in Africa, was foremost a great humanitarian. He was not only dedicated to service in the field of medicine but also an ethical philosopher of his day. In his writings in 1923, he stated his belief that the then-modern civilization was in decay because it lacked the will to love. In a further publication, he encouraged people to adopt a philosophy founded on "reverence for all life." His greatness was revealed through his intrinsic love and compassion toward all forms of life. Although his accomplishments as a philosopher and a humanitarian were highly renowned, his greatest achievement was truly the man behind the work.

Thus, a combination of both qualities is required to reach our highest potential. A woman is not more sensitive if she ignores the reasoning of a situation and goes only by her personal feelings. Feelings alone do not include the reasoning principles that lead to wisdom. Nor is a man more manly when he is strictly intellectual and has no thought for the feelings of those around him. He is limited by an impersonal attitude. The masculine tendency to believe that if something can't be proven, then it doesn't exist is as limiting as the feminine tendency to believe that if something can't be felt, then it can't be true.

Women *and* men need to seek a personal balance for themselves. It isn't a clear-cut case of women needing to add masculine strength and men needing to add a loving energy to their personalities. There are times when the reverse is true. Some women exhibit predominantly masculine qualities just as some men are the embodiment of the compassionate, understanding, and nurturing aspects of the feminine nature. *Balance* is the key.

For women who need to develop more of the masculine or feminine qualities, here are several exercises for generating new characteristics.

Seek out tasks or roles that will require male or female qualities, depending on your needs. To promote masculine aspects, learn something new that enables you to take care of a matter yourself where you once depended upon someone else. Take on a project (start small) and be responsible for fulfilling all aspects of it. Plan it and complete it yourself, rather than depending upon someone else.

To develop feminine qualities of nurturing and mothering, spend time with a small child, animals, or the elderly—they all require a tender and sensitive presence that quietly listens and responds to them. Cook a nice meal for someone or several friends that includes *their* favorite dishes, clean a room and then add something to make it more beautiful, lovingly tend a garden, focus on supporting others in an endeavor that *they* want to do or are interested in, and don't try to take away their control or command unless they ask you to.

Seek to do everyday tasks with an awareness of your energy in how you are approaching them. Do you first look to how it *feels* to do one thing or another? Or do you simply want to get the task done effectively and not become slowed down by emotions?

Decide what elements you want to incorporate into your life, be it focusing more on goals and self-reliance or learning to listen and cooperate with other people. At work you may need to emphasize one aspect more and bring in other elements at home.

Practice being firm, resolute, and unemotional—or sensitive and understanding—depending on what you require.

Watch how you interact with others. Do you focus compassionately on their feelings and personal realities or on the results of your interaction?

If you are too emotional or too sensitive to other people and your surroundings, try to focus more strongly on the goal, or what you are trying to achieve. Not all people can relate to the feelings of a situation. They may need to think it through to come to their own conclusions. Feelings may interfere or hinder the efficient use of a person's time.

Or if you tend to be too masculine, or focused on the outcome of your interactions, try to be more gentle and sensitive with the words you use and the way you offer direction or guidance. Remember to ask how other people are doing and not just go straight to the issue at hand. A blunt approach is too harsh for some people to receive and will turn them against you rather than allow them to offer you their support.

Outwardly attire yourself in a way that helps keep you in balance. For the too-feminine woman, make sure that you are not attired or bedecked in a way that renders you helpless to do things for yourself. For example, extremely high heels are not only hard on your feet but they are nearly impossible to navigate in quickly or efficiently, and wearing very tight, short skirts makes sitting gracefully difficult and sometimes embarrassing. Sometimes weakness is equated with femininity. Do exercises that add some physical strength, which will contribute to your sense of feeling capable.

If you are naturally more masculine-oriented, try giving more attention to your appearance. Incorporate feminine touches such as wearing dresses more frequently, adding earrings or other jewelry to even casual outfits, having your hair cut attractively, and maybe applying a subtle perfume, a bit of makeup, lipstick, or nail polish to give yourself a more feminine look and feel. This does not mean that you must spend an hour arranging your hairdo or walk around in layers of lace. You aren't likely to be comfortable wearing a sea of feminine accoutrements. Add those elements that won't mask *who* you are but enhance what you have.

Seeking balance heightens awareness of oneself and all of creation. Balance leads to a harmonious, fulfilling life. But don't equate "harmonious" with "dull." Seeking to find one's inner point of balance is one of the most exciting parts of living—because it always brings new and intriguing personal challenges. The energy is always shifting, until we reach the perfect balance of a universal, ever-expanding consciousness.

Kindness, compassion, and tenderness bring comfort to all. But discrimination, too, is necessary to assess *when* to give compassion. The woman who is out of balance on the side of "qualities of the heart" may give misplaced compassion or support to others even when they are acting wrongly or cruelly toward another. This is typified by the mother who feels that her own children can do no wrong and supports or excuses their actions no matter what they are. I think that we have all seen it happen. The "blinded," unreasonable mother fiercely supports her child—who eventually becomes a monster of arrogance because he gets away with virtually anything. This is not a display of kindness, compassion, and tenderness on the part of the undiscriminating mother. It would be much kinder to guide the child to act rightly in a situation, to bring out his higher nature. The unreasonable mother can't distinguish between right and wrong actions because she is relying solely on the feelings of the heart without an astute use of the powers of the mind.

On the other side, if a woman is too cerebral and uses only her analytical capabilities, she, too, will be out of balance. Imagine a child who comes running up to his mother with a tear-stained face and clothes covered in dirt, and the mother immediately responding by scolding the child for being clumsy and ruining his clothes. What the child may need most of all is comfort and compassion, not a lecture. This example can be developed a step further. After the comforting warmth of motherly love, the child will likely be more open to guidance, if it is sensitively given. Words of advice are more easily heard once emotions have been calmed.

Discrimination, when untempered by the feelings of the heart, is cold and uncaring. Kindness, compassion, and tenderness reach their full potential when augmented by reason or discrimination. The blending of the feminine traits with the masculine brings out the best in both.

The route to an increased awareness and attunement to grace is unique to each individual. The illustration on page 30 lists feminine and masculine qualities and shows the ways they are experienced in their highest forms. It requires uniting any one feminine quality with any one masculine quality to bring each quality to its fullest expression. Here are a few examples to help you use the illustration as a guide: If you wish to experience intuition, and you are a very "receptive" person, you may need to add "concentration" to bring you the experience of deep intuition. Or, if you naturally feel "receptive," you may need to be "convinced of the rightness of your ideas" to give you the confidence to listen to the intuition you are receiving. For the spiritually inclined person, the quality of "love" coupled with "a broad, impersonal view" will expand to unconditional love, where all people are seen equally as children of God.

The illustration can also be used as a guide on how to correct too strong a tendency. For example, a person who is too "analytical" may want to add "servicefulness" to bring on the quality of wisdom, joy, or respect for all life. Seek balance by developing the opposite trait of that which is most natural or instinctive to you so that you can reach the heights of inner joy, unconditional love, peace, and a life lived to your own highest potential.

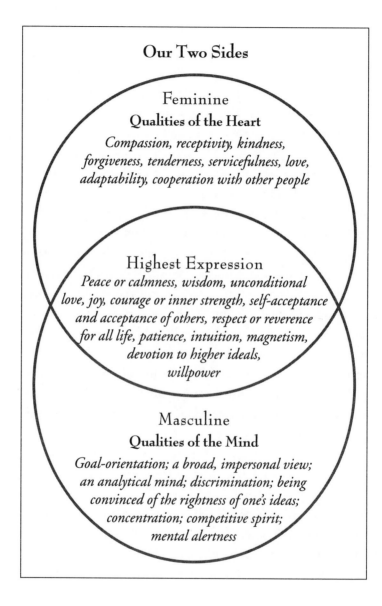

Our Two Sides

Feminine
Qualities of the Heart

*Compassion, receptivity, kindness,
forgiveness, tenderness, servicefulness, love,
adaptability, cooperation with other people*

Highest Expression
*Peace or calmness, wisdom, unconditional
love, joy, courage or inner strength, self-acceptance
and acceptance of others, respect or reverence
for all life, patience, intuition, magnetism,
devotion to higher ideals,
willpower*

Masculine
Qualities of the Mind

*Goal-orientation; a broad, impersonal view;
an analytical mind; discrimination; being
convinced of the rightness of one's ideas;
concentration; competitive spirit;
mental alertness*

The Serviceful Nature of Women

Seeing one's actions or work as a service to others is challenging for many women. There are memories or fears of being dominated that create rigid barriers to giving freely of oneself. This is an unfortunate side effect caused by people illusing personal power over one another. Giving in a serviceful manner, in this negative regard, can seem only a step away from the servile demeanor that was expected in the past from social inferiors, women, servants, and slaves. In years gone by, service to others came to mean a job for the lower classes and was something to be avoided if at all possible. Rarely was respect given to a waitress, secretary, maid, nanny, or cook. It became popular to be concerned only with one's self or family and to think a person foolhardy who gave of his time and energy freely and willingly to others.

Yet service to others is a vast window to selflessness, a deeply spiritual quality.

Mother Teresa gave of herself to the destitute in Calcutta, India, a service she felt was of the highest importance. The throbbing needs of the multitudes constantly called to her, and her service to them became her pathway to God.

It is a noble service that improves the lives of others or helps them change their own lives for the better. This is easier to see on a broad scale than when the ideal of service is brought into the narrower confines of one's own home or line of work.

At home, with friends, at work, and in society, grace is typified by a generosity of spirit: a parent who lovingly sees to the needs of a child; a spouse or partner who willingly gives to a relationship and doesn't measure precisely how much is received in exchange; friends who show real caring for one another and who don't bolt at the first sign of having to give of their love, time, and energy.

Giving to and caring for another person or group of people expands our personal reality to include the happiness of others. It doesn't *exclude* our own happiness; it enhances it. To receive energy, we first must give energy. To receive love, we must give love. It doesn't work if we wait until we get our share and then give a little in return. That's a backward approach, and it will take an eternity before the abundance of grace will enter and fill a life lived without action but filled with the dream that something good might happen.

A great magnetism builds when we lovingly, dynamically, and with great concentration channel our energy out into the world or into a spiritual life. It doesn't matter if it is an outpouring of love for people, business, an ideal, or any creative venture—it is the spirit behind the giving that matters. This tremendous outward flow brings such a feeling of inspiration that it ceases to matter if we get anything in return. It is exhilarating in itself. And when we give selflessly, we also receive abundance. The abundance may be monetary or it may be through an inner transformation, but everyone who has experienced this flow of grace agrees that it is the most deeply fulfilling experience of their lives. Service to others goes far beyond a woman bringing the man of the house his slippers and pipe.

~

Gracious Independence for Women

Two women in my life were the main influence in teaching me about grace with an independent attitude, each in a different way. The first was my mother. The second was our longtime housekeeper, whom I consider my other mother.

My mother led the traditional life of a woman raising her family in a pleasant suburban neighborhood, yet she was very independent-minded. She clearly made her own decisions in various matters, along with choosing what was most important to her personal and family life. She was typical on the outside but held an inner independence.

My mother felt that a woman needs to give to her family, and cooking was one way she expressed her love. She had breakfast ready each weekday morning: The fruit was on the table, the plates warming in the oven, and a hot meal all prepared to start off our day. It never occurred to me that there was any other way for a mother to be. In the evenings, she always greeted my father at the door with a kiss. Then they went together to the kitchen where my father prepared snacks and drinks, and they settled down for their version of cocktail hour while my mother prepared our dinner. My sister and I were always welcome to come and go as we pleased while my mother cooked. She was a wonderful cook, and her presence in the kitchen lent a stable element to all our lives.

This traditional appearance of conformity overlaid my mother's spirit of adventure, her intelligent mind, her strength of character, the emotional support she gave her family, and her contributions of administrative skills to many different organizations dedicated to helping people. These qualities, which were comfortably familiar to her family and close friends, displayed my mother's expansive outlook, her creative search for solutions to any problems, her dynamic yet considerate nature, and her contentment. My mother's independence was manifest in her way of viewing and approaching life, rather than in outwardly "going her own way."

Now, we also had a housekeeper who came to our home five days a week to clean and do the laundry. Flora first came to us when I was only five years old and didn't retire from her job until I went away to college. She was like a second mother to me, and she still fondly calls me her other daughter. I love her dearly and did so from early on. When I was seven, I asked her if she would "be my mother when my mother dies." My mother wasn't ill, so it surprised Flora that I would think of such a thing. Many years later, shortly after my mother died, she told me about that day. Flora never forgot, because she knew that I meant it.

For my entire childhood, I happily followed Flora all around the house and many days would walk with her to the bus stop to see her off. During these hours together, Flora taught me much that guides me to this day.

Flora is one of the most dignified women that I have ever known. She taught me my first lessons about being independent. My mother was very independent in many ways, but Flora knew independence in other ways.

Flora left her first husband for what she considered due cause and was not willing to go back even though he periodically asked her to remarry him throughout the remainder of his life. When she left her second husband, she simply packed a couple of suitcases, took the hand of her young son, and walked out the door leaving everything—the house, the furniture, mementos...everything. She and her son got on a bus together and left for the West Coast. I can't imagine the courage that took.

During my upbringing, I saw Flora as a determined woman who had a quiet dignity, integrity, courage, and a love for God that she didn't speak much about but expressed through her actions. She was tough in spirit; nobody in his right mind would mess with Flora. And she treated me with a depth of love and acceptance that I carry with me to this day. She was always there for me. She was a no-nonsense woman, but she never had to raise her voice to be heard or to get me to obey. She would know every time I did something I wasn't supposed to do. There was no fooling her.

Just a few years ago, Flora came to our home for a vacation. It was a special treat for her as well as for my husband and me, as Flora lives several states away. While she was with us, we had some friends and their son over for dinner. At the end of the meal, the mother turned to her son and gently said, "Mark, you had better go home and do your homework." His response was, "Oh...I don't have to do it." Flora merely said in her matter-of-fact way, "Oh, so you've got the kind of homework you don't gotta do?!" Now, how can anyone answer that one? Well, a few minutes later, that boy excused himself politely and got up from the table to go home and do his homework. You should have seen the surprised expression on all our faces. I suddenly understood how Flora managed to get me to behave—she knew how to say something in such a clear and straightforward manner that there was no way to get around it. She didn't try to finagle, manipulate, or coerce me into behaving a particular way—she inspired cooperation. When she caught me trying to avoid something, she didn't yell or scold. She just let me know, calmly, that she knew what I was up to—as though my avoidance was quite natural but ineffective. I eventually would come around, even if it took her (or me) a few tries. It always worked, which is remarkable.

Flora often told me how important it is to not be dependent on any man, to "make sure you can stand on your own." I took this advice to heart and still find it sad to see a woman suddenly on her own, who doesn't have any means of taking care of herself and doesn't even know where to begin. Even if it isn't necessary financially, it is important to learn enough to be able to function on one's own, because it promotes a personal dignity. Arrogance over one's abilities is unpleasant, but dignity is a sign of self-respect. If we don't know how to respect ourselves, we won't be able to learn how to fully respect others.

Flora gave unstintingly of herself to others but retained the independence and ability to take care of herself and her children. My mother gave the same message of the importance of independence through the individual way she managed the household and her outside interests. She offered love, understanding, guidance, support, and encouragement to her family and to all with whom she worked. She, too, was a woman who lived with dignity and grace.

The independence, dignity, personal integrity, sincerity, and love that I witnessed throughout my childhood taught me more about how to rely on myself and act with grace than any finishing school could have done.

Gracious independence can be expressed as self-reliance, through the pursuit of a career, or by any lifestyle that is personally enriching and benefits others. An independent attitude directed into a positive expression that promotes the betterment of oneself, one's society, or the world at large is a noble achievement.

- Focus on balancing the feminine qualities of the heart with the masculine qualities of the mind in order to reach your own highest potential.
- Feel free to make the choice between home and family, family and career, or career according to your own inclinations. You will not find fulfillment leading a life according to the dictates of another.

- Be generous in spirit. Give of yourself first rather than waiting for others to give energy to you.
- Giving energy to others opens the doorway that allows abundance to flood into your life.
- We must give love in order to receive it.
- Independence is an *attitude* that brings inner freedom. It can be expressed through one's thoughts or consciousness as well as through outward actions.
- Dignity, personal integrity, sincerity, love, and respect for oneself and others are all essential elements of grace.

CHAPTER 3

Be True to Yourself

Don't force yourself into a niche because you think that you should fit. Go with your strengths and talents. In this way, you will find whatever you do to be more fulfilling. If your heart isn't in it, you either need to put your love and energy there—or go the route where you do feel drawn.

Part of the time I can live the role of a woman at home, but I feel inwardly restless and discontent when that is my only focus. I am much happier, and feel full of life, when I can pour energy into my other fields of interest as well. I still devote a lot of time to doing things in and around the house—time that I absolutely treasure—but it isn't enough for me.

Conformity or Independence

Sometimes a woman's wishes coincide with the expectations of her family and friends. This circumvents many of the conflicts that women experience. The expectations of others and one's own preferences, however, do not always match. For the lasting happiness of many women, they must choose whether it is more worthwhile to adapt to the expectations of others or to strike out in another direction that they feel inwardly guided to follow. There is no right answer that applies to everyone.

We have to live with the results of any choices we make. Other people can (and mostly do) advise us in their concern for our welfare. We may find it helpful to listen to advice that is considerately given, and then those views can be taken into account along with our own preferences. But we all must learn to make our own decisions and live by them.

The choice to conform is more comfortable for some people—both women and men. The battle or conflicts that can arise if the choice is made to go in a new or unexpected direction may require more emotional energy than one cares to expend.

A woman can find this choice especially difficult to make. Women tend to adapt to emotional situations and may understandably prefer harmony to a clashing of wills. It sometimes takes years for a woman's family and friends to adjust to an unexpected change, if they do so at all. It is necessary for any major decision to be made thoughtfully and well. If the choice is made to conform, however, it can only succeed if that person then willingly and joyfully embraces the chosen direction. Years of resentment from obediently following the dictates of another, against one's own wishes, will not build character—it is more likely to destroy it.

On the other side, it may be worth any amount of strength and resolve in order to claim your inner calling. A woman's self-confidence or knowledge of the rightness of her decision can buoy her resolve and give her much of the necessary emotional support. The choice may or may not please all others. It is helpful to ask oneself, "What is the right thing to do?" as well as, "What do I want to do?" Do the potential gains outweigh the potential losses resulting from the decision? If there is a deep, driving need to change, it may be difficult to ignore. Yet few people, if any, get to do everything exactly the way they want to, without having to take other people into consideration. Each situation represents a unique combination of elements and personalities.

This open door of choice didn't readily exist decades ago. Women were rarely willing, or able, to abandon their established roles in society. Of course, there were always exceptional women who scorned conformity and set out to follow their inner callings. These women have been our heroines, inspiring persistence and fortitude in others. Their example gives permission to other women to follow their own individual pathways through life.

One such woman was my father's cousin Hilda Hempl Heller. She was the lead character in one of my favorite stories that my father would relate about members (both near and distant) of our family.

Hilda was a statuesque woman of commanding personality, with *three* Ph.D.'s (I could always hear the awe in my father's tone of voice). She dedicated her life wholly to the pursuit of her career in zoology.

In the 1920s, Hilda was embarking on expeditions to the Amazon and through the jungles of Africa in search of animals for her studies or to collect them for zoos. Her husband, described as a small, timid man, had a similar vocation. He was a renowned naturalist and explorer and led numerous expeditions to remote regions, ranging from the Galapagos Islands to Africa. While he quested for reptiles and gorillas in the jungles of Africa, Hilda was in pursuit of rodents and other animals. Sometimes the two traveled together as a husband-and-wife team, but my father always hinted that her husband sought (and found) time away from his domineering wife by scheduling separate treks so that he could seek refuge in the leafy jungle homes of the primates.

The last time my father saw Hilda, she had recently returned from South America where she had been scouting for animals for the Chicago Zoo. The hat Hilda wore looked a bit odd, with decorative pieces missing here and there, but she wore it with pride.

Hilda launched into explaining that, during her recent travels, she had captured an agouti, a large member of the rodent family (over 2 feet long), which intrigued her and soon captured her heart. She took the agouti into her room with her wherever she stayed. She couldn't stand to keep him cooped up in his cage and let him wander freely about her bedroom during the night.

The agouti, true to rodent form, loved to gnaw on things

and apparently took special delight in the wooden legs of tables, beds, and chairs. Hilda simply stocked up on wood glue, colored pastes, and a variety of stains to make quick repairs to the furniture so that she could check out of the hotel before the damage was discovered. It didn't matter to her that a leg had been gnawed off a table—she glued it back on, propped it against a wall, and made a hasty retreat with her newfound friend. She was sweetly charmed by the actions of her agouti. (I don't think that my father found Hilda a very sweet personality and was shocked that a "large rat" would bring out this hidden trait.) Wherever Hilda traveled with this endearing rodent, she carried her repair kit, like an indulgent mother.

Eventually, Hilda had to give up the agouti to the zoo, which saddened her immeasurably. She continued to wear her once-fashionable hat, which the agouti had found quite eye-catching, as a keepsake of their time together. Adorning this relic were the gnawed remnants of colorful wooden fruit that had captured the attention of the agouti. The cherries were mostly gone, and the agouti had begun to whittle away earnestly at the larger fruit before his days of sympathetic companionship were over.

This woman did not blend into society, as one can imagine, but she created her own niche in life where she found fulfillment. Even though she lacked many social graces, she was a woman who was respected for her achievements, if not her charm. Yet animals brought out a hidden generosity of spirit that helped her to express compassion and love. She chose her field well, to help balance her predominantly independent, intellectual, and forceful nature. She would never have been content living a quiet, uneventful life—and she didn't bother to try. She followed a path in life that she knew, inwardly, was right for her.

~

Intuition: The Source of Inspiration and Creativity

What is the source for the inspirations that spark interest in new ideas or in fresh ways of viewing life? And how can this source be reached?

Albert Einstein discovered the law of relativity in a flash of intuitive insight. Yet it took many years of work before he was able to substantiate the discovery to other scientists.

Great composers of the past—Mozart, Beethoven, Bach, Brahms, and Handel, for example—all spoke of the source of their inspirations as a vast consciousness, greater than themselves. These composers listened inwardly to this source for the notes and melodies that flowed into their consciousness and into their great works of music.

There is widespread acknowledgment that thoughts are universally rooted. If one person has a strong idea, it is likely to be picked up by others in the world. General trends, creative ideas, inventions, and an increased consciousness in society all have their source in this energy, in thought.

This universal energy, underlying and inspiring our conscious thoughts, is the essence of grace. Attunement with grace begins with knowledge. Then, if there is an openness, this knowledge unfolds to an increased awareness and deeper understanding. By stages, if not in an intuitive flash, all of us can learn to tap into grace. By learning to listen inwardly, everyone can experience grace—in all of life's endeavors.

How can we learn to use our intuition to get answers to our problems or know what direction is right for us to take?

Attunement with grace begins with knowledge.

Our lives are often crowded with people and events, which makes it difficult to notice our fleeting thoughts. We need to sit calmly, ask our questions clearly, and be receptive with our hearts' feelings to whatever answers come to us.

Here is a practice that will help you experience your intuition. Be sure to read through the entire procedure before beginning so that you have a better understanding of the steps before you start.

First, you need to find a quiet spot in order to be more aware of your inner voice. Choose a place where you can be alone and undisturbed.

Sit in a chair or cross-legged on the floor if you prefer. Sit upright with your back straight, shoulders slightly back, chest in a slightly uplifted position, and chin parallel to the floor. Place your hands in your lap at the junction of the thighs and abdomen, with the palms facing upward. This position will help you to relax yet still maintain an erect posture.

Close your eyes to shut out visual distractions. Take deep, even breaths to calm and center yourself. Inhale and exhale through the nostrils only, if you can, as this is more calming to the mind and body than breathing through the mouth.

Inhale slowly and fully, mentally counting from one to eight; hold your breath for eight counts; then gradually exhale all the air, counting from one to eight mentally. Repeat the cycle, beginning the next breath *without pausing after the exhalation*. Keep your attention focused on your breath as it flows through your nostrils into your lungs, is held, and flows out again. Breathe in with a sense of peace filling your body; then cast out scattered thoughts or worries with your exhalation so that you can focus single-mindedly on your question. Do this breathing exercise three or more times, until your mind is peaceful and focused. (You may inhale, hold, and exhale for up to the count of 12, if you can do so without any strain. The three parts of the exercise should each be for the same number of counts—inhale eight, hold eight, exhale eight; or to counts of 12.)

Be clear about what you want to ask. "What do you think?" is not a clear question. Keep your question short, but detailed. "Should I continue my present career?" If it is an either/or situation, think of the choices as two distinct options and ask them as separate questions. Phrase each question so that it can be answered with a yes or no. It will be easier to understand the response. You may even want to write your question or questions on paper that you can hold in your upturned hands, to make it more tangible. And, most of all, be willing to receive with an open heart whatever answer does come. It may not be the answer you want, or expect. Your intuition can't give you a clear answer if you ask, "Should I continue my present career—I really don't want to, I can't stand it, and you can't mean that I should do that." You must be impartial and ask honestly and sincerely.

To ask your question: Keep your eyes closed. Lift one hand in front of you and gracefully reach up and out in front of your forehead with your palm uplifted. Place your inner gaze at that point and visualize your question there as though floating in a clear bubble. You may want to relax your hand back into your lap once you have your inner gaze at that point—or you can raise and reach outward with *both* your hands to the point in front of your forehead, hold your palms upward, and imagine your question resting in your hands. Concentrate on one question, "Should I...?" Focus on the question until you feel it has been clearly made. Ask with deep attention.

To receive your answer: Touch both hands at the center of your chest at the heart area, where feelings dwell. Place your fingertips at that center, then in a graceful motion, open your arms as though you are throwing open the doors to your heart. Hold your arms outward in a comfortable position, as if holding open the doors, and turn your palms upward to be more receptive. Listen to the answer with the openness of your heart. The heart is your receiving center. Think "yes" to your question and see if you feel an answering, pleasing resonance in your heart, like a vibrational wave filling your heart. That means "yes." If you feel a slight disturbance, or emotional discomfort, that means "yes" is *not* the answer. Think "yes" and "no" several times to be sure of the response.

If you feel nothing, then think "no" to your question. Do you get a strong corresponding feeling in your heart as if saying, "You're right"? Ask again several times to recheck the answer.

What do you do if it is a two-part question? First, ask one question clearly and see if you can get a clear "yes" or "no" response. Then ask the second half of the question, "Should I do this other thing...?" Repeat the whole process of holding up the question to your higher self and being open to the response in your heart. The arm movements will not be necessary once you have learned the feeling of how to ask and receive answers, but they are beautiful gestures that help us attune ourselves to the energy flow of grace. You may get a more definite answer when asking this second part of the question.

And what about the times when you feel nothing? Go ahead and start acting on one of the specific choices. "Do I, or don't I?" may become more clear once you put out energy in one direction. Then the answer may come with an uneasy feeling that you shouldn't be doing that. Continue to ask, even as you act. The universe does respond, but we have to listen. And remember to keep checking. The answer may be "yes" for a while, but you may need to alter that course of action in the future. "Yes" is not always forever.

One other point to be aware of is that we sometimes get a positive response, follow that course of action, and then fail at what we are trying to do. Does that mean we have goofed up?

Was our intuition wrong? If the question was clearly asked, and the answer received impartially, then, no, our intuition was right. It just may be that through our failure the next step can open to us in a way that would not have been possible if we attained immediate success. We may need to learn something, or the right timing may be different than our own conception of it. Don't give up if your intuition is strongly guiding you. You will gain much more if you follow the advice of your higher self, or the Spirit within. We have a time frame that we personally want, but there is also the rhythm of the universe.

The president of France, Jacques Chirac, lost two elections for presidency before he won the office after his third campaign. It was right for him to be president, but not for 14 years after his first attempt. But he gained knowledge and experience through the course of events that eventually brought him to success. He didn't give up, as he obviously felt that it was the right thing for him to do.

Listening to Intuition

It takes courage, willpower, and determination to follow our own beliefs. So if you don't get the results you expected, and you still feel guided strongly, you will have to learn when to trust your inner voice. The more you practice using your intuition, the faster and easier it is to recognize its presence. Soon, you'll find that solutions to problems, answers to baffling questions, and guidance in the direction of your life can come through this channel.

When I receive strong guidance, I experience it as almost a blow to the chest, like a sound wave striking my body. I can't ignore it—it is absolutely clear about what it is telling me to do. It silently prods me to comply. I may not have any idea why I'm supposed to go in that direction, but I take that course of action anyway. And it has always been rewarding in the long run in knowledge gained, fresh insights, and unforeseen success.

People like Einstein learn how to work with their intuition to plumb the secrets of the universe. One of my favorite quotes of his is "I want to know God's thoughts...the rest are details." A great part of his genius was in a gift for being able to focus with intense concentration on what he wanted or needed to know, for remaining completely receptive to whatever answer he received, and for knowing the answer that did come was the right one for that moment. And he never stopped questioning.

~

Awaken the True Self That Resides within You

Our true self is our higher self. Who wants to dwell forever on their lower or negative qualities? It doesn't improve a negative quality to contemplate it endlessly. It only reaffirms it until the time when it can be transmuted to its opposite, or higher, expression.

The way to the higher expression is to magnetize the positive quality you do want to develop or strengthen. An increase in energy—be it for the positive or negative element—will draw more energy to itself. The greater the increase in energy or magnetism, the greater the change or enhancement. This focused energy or magnetism can work for us or against us. It is one reason that people often can't seem to get out of a particular pattern of behavior.

I am always inspired by the determination of a close friend of ours and the extraordinary transformation in his life. David decided one day that he wanted to be a runner. He did not have a naturally athletic build, nor was he already trim and fit. There he was, a man in his late forties, sitting at a desk all day long, who occasionally went for a slow jog where he ran a quarter-mile, rested a bit, and jogged back.

He and his wife were on a vacation with a group of friends when a few of the men asked David to join them for an easy run, which sounded like fun. But his friends were all marathon runners, and he felt extremely humiliated by the way they cruised along with ease while he was struggling to keep up. He resolved to change himself.

David's schedule was busy, so he got up at 4:00 A.M. daily to start training on his own. He ran up hills and down, chugging along up the steep parts. His strength and endurance grew as the weeks passed by. After a few months, he went on a run with his neighbor and role model, John, who was a marathon and ultramarathon runner (runs of 50 miles or longer) with many years of racing experience. The two men took to a long, flat road, and for the first time in his life, David felt the rhythm of running. It was a beautiful experience.

David kept to his training and was prodded on by comments from John. He ran the 7-mile Bay-to-Breakers race in San Francisco, then months later, a half-marathon. Finally, he ran his first marathon just over a year after he decided to get into shape. But he felt that it was a disaster, even though he finished the entire 26 miles, for his time was slow.

This was his pivotal point. He looked at the elite runners and thought to himself that he really *was* one of them, but trapped (unkindly) in an overweight and out-of-shape body. He united his belief and feelings into a strong inner knowledge that he already was an elite runner, and he suddenly knew what to do and how he needed to train. His running time at the next marathon, six months later, was 1 hour faster than his previous race. He was also 40 pounds lighter than the year before.

David then started getting eager for better running times. He pushed his training harder and began getting injuries, one after another. For the entire year after his great achievement with racing, he could often barely walk, so he started to swim to keep in shape. Then, while he and his wife were vacationing again, he rented a road bike, and he started to add bicycling to his routine. After a couple of months of this new program, he decided to train for a triathlon.

He looked for a swim coach and discovered one in an inspiring woman who had won three Olympic gold medals in swimming and now runs a swim school 80 miles from his home. She taught him how to improve his stroke so well that his swim times dropped phenomenally. He was ready to race.

He celebrated his 50th birthday with his first triathlon just behind him, and a second one coming up. Mechanical problems prevented him from finishing the tough Wildflowers race, but he hoped to complete his next meet.

The second triathlon he entered was the Ultimate Escape, formerly known as Escape from Alcatraz, one of the most difficult races on the mainland, and he finished in the top third. And he's not done yet.

John, David's role model and "constant competition" during his training, no longer teases David to prod him on. They run together, sharing the joy of the rhythm and flowing pace. It is a far cry from three years ago when this all began, with David catching his breath after a quarter-mile jog.

David fixed his eye on his goal and tried continually to feel the energy of what it was like for the people who were best at what he was trying to accomplish. He did everything he could to gain skill and competence and learned from those who excelled at the sport and could convey the right spirit. When he had the setback from his running injuries, he turned his attention to a related activity that would support and round out his previous accomplishments. His energy magnetized the right coach in John, opened a new field with his swimming and biking, and led him to a swimming coach who helped him enormously. But above all, he never gave up. That is how magnetism is created.

First, however, you need to identify the quality that you want to change. This takes extra attention in listening to your own words and ideas.

So often I hear someone (or catch myself) mentioning a negative or limiting trait over and over, deepening its hold on the mind and body. "I can't do *that*!" is commonly uttered even if we have never even attempted whatever it is we think can't be done. It affirms an inability to accomplish new or difficult things, rather than keeping a more open mind about our capabilities. Have you tried? Or tried and failed *once*? Or tried again in a dispirited manner and thus continued to fail? Are you subtly defeating yourself before even beginning?

Another such lament plagues many women in their romantic lives: "I just can't seem to choose the right type of man!" But saying it only reinforces that thought. It is much more helpful to say, "I haven't chosen the right type of man in the past, but I'm going to choose more wisely this time." It affirms a change, not the same old mistake.

"I haven't succeeded yet but will keep trying" is an outlook that can bring ultimate success in any venture. It attunes one's energies with the vast flow of grace. Grace can come to us in the form of good fortune or blessings if we keep open to, and magnetize, its positive flow of energy.

The Power of the Mind

I first understood the power of the mind and how greatly it can effect change when it was demonstrated in my own life. I was an avid downhill ski racer during my high school years. One year, I returned from summer racing camp with high enthusiasm and began my preseason training in July. I trained hard and diligently, 3 to 4 hours every day. In early winter, the snows finally came. Going down my first practice course of the season, I caught a tip on a gate, fell, and tore a tendon and ligaments in my ankle.

I was in a cast until nearly the end of the ski season. I missed skiing tremendously, and under the circumstances, the only way I could enjoy it was by visualizing myself going down the slopes. I added to my mental pictures the many new pointers I had received from the coaches at ski camp. I mentally skied any time of day or night that I felt like it. It was the only way for me to appease my deep longing for the exhilaration of skiing.

My cast was eventually taken off, and I was ready to get back on the slopes the final few weeks of the season. My first day out, I discovered my skiing had improved to such an extent that my coach didn't even recognize me as I made my first enthusiastic runs down the mountain. I couldn't believe the change myself. My coach approached me at the end of the day and asked me how I had managed to improve so dramatically without being able to practice. I told him that I had been skiing in my mind, executing turns over and over again. He was astonished by my answer.

That summer when I returned to racing camp, the coaches there could hardly believe their eyes. They, too, asked how I managed to make such phenomenal progress in my skiing, because they had never seen anyone change so much in just one year. I told them that I did as they had suggested the previous summer and pictured in my mind the way I *should* be skiing. I was unhindered by the actual physical practice, and I never failed to make the turns correctly in my mind. Once my mind "understood," my body simply followed along.

The method was really quite simple and was probably especially effective because I enjoyed it so much. It wasn't a grim practice at all.

First, I decided what I wanted to practice doing—was it left turns or rights? Going through a race course, or making tight turns on a steep slope?

Then I focused on that one aspect. I pictured, and tried to feel, exactly how my weight should be distributed over the skis, what my body position should be like, where my arms and poles should be, and where I needed to be looking. I pictured everything as clearly as possible. Then, I mentally commenced the action, executing slowly and carefully just what I wanted to practice. After slowly going through the motions, I would then speed them up until, eventually, I was "skiing" at normal speed. Sometimes I would vary the scene by giving myself increasingly difficult maneuvers. I tried to feel all the movements as much as picture them.

It was better in some ways than the actual physical practice—I never had to fall at high speeds, ski in freezing temperatures with low visibility, or experience an "off" day. Every day I could mentally ski exactly the way I wanted to—and my body learned how in reality by my focusing clearly, and with deep concentration, on the actions I wished to be experiencing. I had no idea that my thoughts were actually making any changes. It wasn't until I was back on the slopes that I realized the importance of what I had been doing.

This technique can be applied to anything. Some people dread activities such as public speaking and can work on visualizing themselves facing the situation with confidence and with just the approach they wish to make. Or the technique can be used in learning a new skill. Possibly you want to change a tendency toward losing your temper at a spouse or children at the end of the day when you're tired and patience is at a low point. Concentrate deeply on positive, helpful, or kind ways to react to others.

The main steps of visualization are: 1. Be clear about what you want to change or improve; 2. Mentally picture and try to feel yourself (physically or emotionally) in the situation; 3. Focus your attention on as many details as you comfortably can (you can always add in more details later); and 4. Concentrate deeply and calmly on performing the desired action perfectly.

The process should bring you a good feeling of success. Don't let any disappointments about not having been able to accomplish something successfully in the past creep into your imagery—except to teach yourself how to overcome the difficulties. Learn and do everything you can to support your willingness and desire toward change. Even during my months off the slopes, I still needed to work on staying in good physical condition so my body would be ready and able to ski once my injury had healed sufficiently.

Using mental imagery is a fabulous way to learn to change old ways of doing things—be it the habits of negative thoughts, emotional behavior, or physical habits.

Say "Yes!" to Life
without Giving Yourself Away

Women tend to be naturally adaptive to life and the needs of others. They can give and give and give until there is nothing left. "What about me?!" is the woman's belated refrain, as she is left bewildered and somewhat stunned that no one took care of *her*.

Who hasn't given energy in some way, resented it, and then, compulsively, done it again? "I can't believe that I did that again!" is a frustrating feeling for everyone. Eventually, though, the same mistakes become less frequent, until they are replaced with a new way of handling an old situation.

Enjoy Being You

It seems as though it should be easy to know your own self—but that is possibly the most challenging discovery we each have to make. Who we are isn't a matter of blond hair or brown, light skin or dark. The essence of who we are is subtle and played out through our actions. Then, too, who we are, and how we interact with the world, can change over time, showing us a side of ourselves and of others that we never suspected was there.

I was first faced with deeply questioning my own inner nature when I was in my twenties and acting both as a balloon pilot and fulfilling the social role of my recently deceased mother. I couldn't tell if I was pretending to be one thing socially and was really another or if I was truly in tune with both. Was I behaving solely in accordance with my father's wishes or following my own inclinations? Emotions can be so difficult to sort out.

Some days would begin before sunrise with a long drive into the country to a launch site for the balloon. After the exciting process of inflating the colorful, 75-foot balloon, one or two passengers would join me in the wicker basket, and we would begin a leisurely flight over fields and pastures, pine-scented woods, and rolling hills, with snow-capped mountains lending a serene backdrop to the peaceful setting.

These adventurous travels by balloon—going with the winds, gracefully drifting over field and farm—came to an abrupt end after the balloon had landed and it was time to pack it up.

And balloons are heavy! My four propane tanks weighed over 70 pounds each, and the fabric alone weighed over 230 pounds; then there was the burner, the basket, ropes, and more. The whole ensemble, when packed into the basket, was more than 450 pounds. Occasionally, my friend Sylvia and I had to get the balloon into the trailer by ourselves. It was a lot of hard work. And there was also the dirt factor.

Whatever was in the field where the balloon landed and deflated became caught in, or smeared on, the fabric of the balloon. To pack the balloon away, 1,000 yards of nylon had to be grabbed, dragged, and shoved into a giant stuff-bag in the wicker basket. There was no delicate way to avoid whatever was coating the fabric. It wasn't at all bad when it was only some grassy stubble or remnants from a cultivated crop, but we weren't always that lucky.

I vividly remember the first dairy farmer I met, who burst out laughing when he saw my look of shocked disbelief at the sight of what 100 or so unconcerned cows will leave in a field. "Cow pies" is an accurate description of the size of these bovine gifts back to nature. They happened to be in the field where the balloon lay deflated on the ground. Needless to say, some days, I wasn't too tidy when I finally returned home.

The experience of these sunrise flights was often in great contrast to the rest of the day's events. Many times the flights were followed by an evening with my father at the symphony, theater, or opera. I would dash home from the day's flight, clean up, dispose of any remnants from the customer's champagne picnic, cook dinner, adorn the proper attire for the evening, and off I would go with my father to sit quietly and enjoy the evening's entertainment, as though it was the most natural thing for me to do. Yet these two activities felt worlds apart.

It was challenging to make the shift from one part of my life to the other. Eventually—and it took a while—I realized that I did, in fact, feel comfortable in both worlds. I actually *wasn't* just pretending to fit in with my father's social world—I enjoyed it. I also loved, and was thoroughly devoted to, my outdoor life. The conflict wasn't in the two disparate elements, just in my belief that I should only do, or be, one thing or another.

Of course, we can manifest more than one interest or direction or more than one way of being. This is often what helps to balance our personalities and allows the development of various talents. What do we enjoy? And where do we feel ill-at-ease—and why?

We all end up having to go against our natures from time to time—but for an entire lifetime? The attempt to repress our inner nature continually, and not guide it into a compatible course, usually results in our dramatically catapulting out of the formerly adopted lifestyle and going to the other extreme in a desperate attempt to escape the old ways.

We each have our own specific nature—be it dynamic and outgoing, timid and thoughtful, studious and diligent, playful and social, or any imaginable combination of qualities. If you are dynamic and outgoing, don't try to hide behind a meek voice and submissive posture. It won't change those dynamic qualities—it just creates a cloud of confusion that rarely succeeds in deceiving others, or yourself. Pretending the dynamic quality isn't really there at all won't bring growth, self-understanding, and self-acceptance. It is much more productive and satisfying to work with individual qualities or strengths and put to use the desirable aspects.

A dynamic personality has lots of energy. That energy can be channeled into any direction—even into becoming dynamically compassionate or receptive to other people's ideas and ways of being.

What if you feel timid rather than dynamic? If you feel timid or helpless, you are not alone. Even very dynamic, successful women experience times of doubt and insecurity—they just learn how to get through them, or rise above them.

Insecurity is experienced by women and men alike. A way

to learn how to get through this feeling is to try new things that you feel you can succeed in. This will help you develop a growing confidence and a "yes" approach to life.

Start by changing some of your responses. "I don't know how" can imply that you also don't intend to try or are too afraid to make an attempt. Instead, add to your response, "Can you show me?" or "I'd be happy to try, but I haven't done that before." Mentally change your thoughts so they will accept new situations and challenges. "I'll try" can then grow into "Oh, I'll do that!" It empowers you with the ability to learn and explore your potential.

If you feel timid or shy under "normal" conditions (normal to others, that is), give yourself a pep talk to gain self-confidence, courage, and determination so it will help you follow through with the action. Tell yourself you *can*. Or, you can certainly try. No one feels confident in *all* situations.

A quick exercise to develop a positive outlook and enthusiasm is to swing both arms outward from your chest with your hands in fists until they are straight out to the side from your shoulders—and say out loud with this gesture, "I am *positive*!" Bring your hands back to your chest and immediately thrust them straight forward, saying, "*energetic*!" Then bring your hands back again to your chest to be thrust straight above your head with your hands opening as you say, "*enthusiastic*!" Now try it as one whole affirmation as you make the arm movements—"I am *positive, energetic, enthusiastic*!" Give the words energy as you say them. Do three rounds of this for a quick pick-me-up—you'll feel much more ready to face what's ahead.

It's perfect to do when no one is watching, but if someone does see you, you may end up teaching it to them once they witness the results!

Then, once you have given yourself a boost, take full, deep breaths that draw energy into your body and mind; stand up straight with good posture to increase the look of confidence; walk or sit with an awareness of energy rather than taking hesitant steps or sitting with a meek or fearful expression—and go out and do the best you can. No one is perfect, including the people in the situation you have to face.

Success may not always be yours, but no one succeeds in anything they never attempt to do. Try to accept any failures as important steps needed for future victories. It is better to try your best and fail than to allow the fear of defeat to stop all attempts.

You should also focus on your positive inner qualities of sensitivity, kindness, compassion, or love in order to magnetize and build those quiet strengths and build inner confidence, courage, and feelings of self-worth. There is no need to advertise your weaknesses—build on your strengths. The weaknesses will lessen and transform into sturdy attributes over time.

Often, all that is required to face challenges, insecurity, and timidity is extra energy to help you through an ordeal.

What Social Type Are You?

We can take hints about our own natures from our outer realities as well as our inner perceptions. Just our way of functioning in society can help guide us in a general fashion.

The Social Person

There are many who love having an active social life. For this type of person, lots of activity and groups of people mean fun and good times. This person looks forward to the next gathering and comes to life in the midst of social activities. If this is your demeanor, you will probably excel in your social interactions with lots of different people. "Why have quiet evenings at home when there is something else to do?" may be your general outlook on life.

Interactions that are reduced to only one other person may feel slightly awkward to you, eliciting an instinctive desire to cast about for more people to include in the conversation. Including others in social activities is your forte—and is much appreciated by those who maybe feel excluded or neglected otherwise.

Yet if you are a strongly social person, you are likely to have a terrible time trying to live a solitary life. It goes too much against your innate love of people and gatherings. You may glow in this lively element yet wither away in solitude.

The One-on-One Person

Some people are outstanding in their dealings with others on a one-on-one basis and enjoy spending time with people—but put them in a crowd and they are at a loss. In a large group, they may want to either retreat into a corner, snag one person and stick to them for the duration, or try to bluff their way through the ordeal. If you feel a strong satisfaction in connecting with people in a deep or meaningful way, this may be the avenue for expressing your inner nature. Even if you are in a conversation with more than one other person, there is likely to be a desire to connect deeply with each individual.

If you are most comfortable in a one-on-one situation, it helps to acknowledge your nature and not berate yourself for it. Rather than try to force yourself to love a large party, try to stay more with smaller gatherings, or your specialty, the one-on-one interaction. When you are not able to make a choice, simply buddy-up at a large gathering. Surely there are others who feel as you do.

Do you feel overcome with shyness or terribly awkward? The trick is to get your energy moving outward, away from yourself. If you are more concerned about someone else, you will have less time to focus on your own uncertainty.

Graciousness and good manners are a great crutch in a large gathering. Grace endorses greeting people in a friendly fashion, talking with other people, and asking about things they enjoy doing. In essence, it gets your energy flowing toward others. If you allow your thoughts and feelings to retreat into yourself, you will only feel more shy and insecure. Just knowing this can help you to monitor your ability to function well in a group.

It has been considered gracious not to take up too much of one person's time at a party. Social mingling amongst a crowd is an art that you can learn.

Act as though everyone is a friend, even if you have never met before. This attitude welcomes conversation and a sense that you belong and feel accepted. Your openness will also be evident to others who are looking for someone to talk to. You may end up having such a great time that you hate to leave the party!

Conversations in large gatherings are prone to be shorter than if you are in a more intimate setting. Be aware that people who are more social types follow a rhythm of talking a little with one group and then wandering off to visit a bit elsewhere—and they have no intention of allowing the conversation to become too deep or involved—they have people to see.

Social gatherings generally require a lighter exchange, not weighed down with intense or highly controversial matters. For those of you who would like to feel more equipped to handle social dialogue, there are a number of books available on the topic of how to talk with people in all situations.

What should you do if someone is rude or insulting to you? Unfortunately, not everyone has good manners. Try to ignore the unpleasant comment as best as you can, politely say, "Excuse me," and move on to converse with someone else as though it is a natural thing to do. You are not obligated to explain your actions in a social setting, and it is customary to mingle with different people. You can tell the person that you will talk it over later, if you must say anything. "Making a scene" is unpleasant for everyone present. A neutral response will diffuse the situation as well as maintain harmony within the larger group.

The Solitary Type

The solitary person has a deep need for time on his own. Friends and family may be very important to him, but he needs time away from the distractions of people to recharge himself.

If you are a solitary type, you may delight in working and/or living on your own or living in a remote area, and you are likely to prefer most evenings at home, in order to recharge for the next day. People may be an invaluable and cherished part of your life—just not *all* of the time.

It is much easier for the solitary person to enjoy small gatherings, or a one-on-one conversation, than a large group or gathering. The problem isn't with the variety of individuals as much as the sheer magnitude of the numbers. If you are a person who relishes having quiet time alone, be like the one-on-one and try the buddy system at the next gathering you attend. It will usually help if you can connect with someone in a meaningful way.

Some solitary types, too, find it helpful to give energy to the group, like helping serve food or drinks or seeing that a particular guest is well-cared-for and enjoying the party. It can help make conversation feel more natural and offers you a means for connecting with the other guests and overcoming shyness. You may feel more at ease if you have a sense of purpose or usefulness. Remember, as with the one-on-one person, keep energy going out to other people and use graciousness as your guide. If you know the person well who is hosting the event, you may want to ask if you can assist him in some way—he may appreciate the help if it isn't a fully catered event. And tips for the one-on-one type will work great for you, too.

~

Is One Social Type Better Than Another?

Naturally, people can blend the qualities of a solitary type with a more social type and can comfortably stretch toward being a little more one way or the other. Yet identifying our own nature helps relieve unrealistic expectations we may be placing on ourselves. These tendencies are not faults that need correcting—they are simply reflective of our inner nature.

It is hard for the socially oriented person to understand how anyone can stand to be away from friends or colleagues for any length of time, but it is equally difficult for the solitary person to understand the social life of the person who adores being with people day after day, night after night. These different types of people may be great friends, but they won't want to lead the same life. It is harder for couples to work around this if they are at opposite ends of the spectrum, but understanding the differences helps transform any blame, into acceptance.

- Don't try to force yourself into a niche because you think that you should fit. Go with your strengths, your talents.

- If you choose to conform to the wishes of another, then willingly and joyfully embrace the chosen direction.

- If you choose to pursue a course of action that goes against the wishes of those close to you, then be sure to ask yourself, "What is the right thing to do?" as well as "Do the gains outweigh the losses?"

- Learn to use your intuition wisely. It can lead to the source of creativity and inspiration, solutions to problems, and an increase in awareness or under-standing.

- Seek to experience a life that will bring true inner harmony and fulfillment.
- Verbalize your thoughts in a positive manner to help magnetize a desired change.
- Harness the power of the mind through positive thinking to learn new things or ways of being.

CHAPTER 4

~

Rediscovering Grace

Sit up straight! Look people in the eyes when you are talking to them. Say 'Please' and 'Thank you.' Don't just flop down in a chair—sit down and stand up gracefully. Be polite...and don't interrupt!"

These are some of the social criteria that are associated with grace or graciousness. Persistent reminders of the guidelines to "correct" behavior can be annoying at times. The problem is, few of us have been told *why* these social contrivances are beneficial. They have become merely a convention and have lost their connection to their basis in universal truths. In fact, there are deeper principles behind these outward displays of grace.

Coming out of an era when, as recently as my grandmother's time, women were not openly "allowed" to read newspapers, were considered generally lacking in intellectual capabilities (and thus expected to accept their husbands' or fathers' opinions as their own), and were slated to dutifully and obediently serve the men of the household, it isn't much of a surprise that many of the old conventions were tossed out in women's overwhelming desire for freedom and equality. It took a great force of emotional energy to shift those shocking restrictions. And it is to be expected that a lot of resentment and rebellion against imposed customs will accompany any change of that magnitude.

But the outward forms of grace aren't about suppressing one's freedom and equality. When enacted with an awareness of the meaning behind them, the social forms of grace actually benefit us. Many of these conventions are based upon deeper truths, not the shallowness of conformity. It is time to reevaluate the significance of grace so it can be used wisely as a means of increasing one's awareness.

Guidelines of behavior are useful social customs. They help to smooth the way of communication and lessen misunderstandings. With a dissolution of the old customs has come confusion. We have nothing to replace the old and have not yet completely decided on the new. So people act in a nebulous fashion, hoping to interpret correctly the words and gestures of others—or simply demand by their actions that others conform to their own personal standards. This confusion can't be dispelled without some adherence to structure.

My father, a dignified, white-haired gentleman, was thoroughly puzzled one day when he held a door open for a woman who then turned and upbraided him for it. He was quite flustered by her reaction. On his part, it was a customary show of courtesy—and, he said, the door would have shut in the woman's face if he hadn't held it open. Yet the woman obviously felt insulted, taking his action to imply that she was incapable of holding the door open for herself. No wonder this era is perplexing to both men and women! My father asked what was wrong with being courteous. And that sums it up...what *is* wrong with being well-mannered? The action of holding open a door can be done with courtesy, or it can be done with derision. As the recipient of this gesture, it is far more dignified to pretend it is respectful, even if one senses a small gleam of contempt. There are delightful ways to gracefully take the sting out of an insult and turn it to one's own advantage. It is an art women once excelled in, and it will always remain a valuable social skill for those who are gifted in its ways.

The Importance of Good Posture

The physical acts of grace bring a rise in energy and awareness. The more energy and focused attention we command, the more we can change ourselves and our lives. No one can experience more from life without increasing energy. "More" means an increase. If our lives feel empty or unfulfilling, we need to flood those areas that are lacking with greater energy and sensitive awareness. Anything that decreases energy, be it our physical actions or negative thoughts, will only hinder our growth and sense of fulfillment. Raising the positive energy of the body and mind will weaken the hold that negative thoughts and actions have on us. In time, even the most tenacious negative qualities will dissipate, and their energy will turn around, bringing a glorious personal triumph. The small changes are easiest to make first. Then, as these small changes accumulate, it will be easier to tackle the bigger ones.

The posture of standing and sitting up straight actually increases the energy of the body. See for yourself. Slump over as you stand or while sitting in a chair. It is hard to feel dynamic and enthusiastic in this position. Slouched or hunched over, one's energy feels less alert, more downward or drowsy; it is a posture of defeat. It is also nearly impossible to fill the lungs with full, deep breaths of air in this position. This makes it difficult to oxygenate the blood—our bodies' river of life. Just the state of having less oxygen in the body will cause a lethargic energy, and the mind has less oxygen available for quick thinking. One's digestion isn't able to work as well either when constricted by poor posture.

To practice good posture, first, stand up. It is easier to feel the correct position in this pose.

> **The physical acts of grace bring a rise in energy and awareness. The more energy and focused attention we command, the more we can change ourselves and our lives.**

Stand with what feels like a straight spine, your feet several inches apart, or whatever distance is most comfortable for you. Place your weight evenly balanced between both feet. To check that your weight is evenly distributed, slowly lean a little to your left so your weight shifts more to the left foot; feel what that is like. Then move back to the center and lean toward the right, shifting your weight more on the right foot. Feel that position, then again move back to the center. Can you feel the balance more clearly now? Continue by rocking forward to place more weight on your toes and then backward to feel the emphasis on your heels. Locate your central position. Your feet are the foundation of the body, and the way you distribute your weight will affect the rest of your carriage. See if your toes are pointing straight ahead or turned outward or inward. You can gradually try to ease your foot position more toward a straight-ahead orientation. Although toes pointing forward is the ideal, it should not be forced. If you can set them ahead, great—but if you can't do so comfortably, then you can work toward that direction a bit at a time if it matters to you.

Standing with your weight evenly balanced and your spine straightened, see if you have your knees relaxed and softly bent. They won't look bent in a mirror but may feel a little like they are if you are accustomed to the locked stance. Knees should not be locked in place. It isn't healthy to seize up our bodies anywhere.

To position your back, shoulders, and head, raise your upper chest as though being lifted by a string from the ceiling that is attached to a point above your breasts and below your collar bone. This positions your chest and upper back. Now move your shoulders slightly back, arms relaxed and hanging down to your sides—and then briefly push down toward the ground slightly with your hands. That helps put your shoulders in the right position and hold your chest up. Relax the push from your hands; it's just to obtain the right posture initially. Your arms and shoulders should be completely relaxed as you stand.

Keep your chin parallel to the floor. That's it! This is not how I always carried myself—and you may find that the same is true for yourself. Look in a mirror to check on your positioning. Check that you are not holding tension anywhere. When your posture is correct, you may notice a new calm, centered feeling.

Do a quick check: weight evenly distributed between your feet, with them comfortably apart; knees unlocked and relaxed slightly forward; chest uplifted; shoulders back, with arms and shoulders relaxed; neck relaxed with chin parallel to the floor; ankles, hips, and shoulders in a vertical line, with the hips not tilted forward or backward.

If this posture is unfamiliar, you'll find walking like this to be a new experience. Keep your spine, chest, and chin in the correct posture, then walk forward as though being led from your center—the vicinity of the solar plexus, or region between your lower ribs. Your entire body should feel relaxed through the trunk area. You don't want to thrust forward from your breasts or lead yourself with your chin—hold an upright form and move forward with ease and grace. Allow your arms to be relaxed by your sides.

You will feel more confident and centered in your whole being. I found this such an extraordinary experience the first time I walked this way that I kept going up and down the hallway at home, reveling in the change! And while you are walking around, glance down to see if your toes are pointing straight ahead with each step. You can change their angle to a small degree, but don't be drastic. Allow your body to have its quirks and inclinations; we don't all fit the same mold. The goal is not the perfect stance—it is to move toward the direction of good posture to whatever degree we can.

When sitting down, the same elements should be there as when standing: spine straight, chest gently uplifted, and chin level. The difference here is that you may be using your hands and arms, so your shoulders need to move around. With your chest slightly lifted, it should hold the shoulders in straight alignment with your hips. Whether you are standing or sitting, the hips and shoulders should line up. If you lean forward too much, you are likely to be bending from, and straining, your lower back. Remember to check periodically that your shoulders are straight above your hips, and that you are relaxed in this pose. And what about your feet and legs? Try to keep your feet flat on the floor, or cross your ankles if that is more comfortable. You don't want that stiff, uptight, rigid look of the schoolmarms of yesteryear. Take a look at Audrey Hepburn in the later scenes of *My Fair Lady* to see someone who moves with real swanlike grace.

And here is an important tip—don't start trying to pull in your belly; it only causes tension and discomfort everywhere else. The nervous system that governs relaxation *throughout the whole body* runs right through your diaphragm, at the region of your solar plexus. If that area is tense, so is the rest of you! A calm, centered posture is far better for you than trying to hold everything in. Do you truly care so much about how slender you look that you're willing to sacrifice your health and well-being? How much admiration do you have for a person who identifies *who* she is with her waist size? In fact, our good posture will actually aid our digestion—and our health—so we can end up being more svelte after all! Hopefully, our society will add *that* aspect to our improvements over the Victorian age!

I learned a lovely phrase from the teacher of the Ananda Yoga Training Program. He encourages his students to bring harmony to their whole beings by complementing good posture with "a relaxed belly, expanded heart, and soft eyes." This way we can be calm, centered, and view the world with love and kindness. That is truly the correct posture for all of our lives!

Good physical and mental health rely in large part on our adherence to a posture that allows the free flow of life-giving energy throughout the body. We cannot neglect the body and expect the mind to remain healthy and alert. It is much more difficult to remain positive and dynamic in outlook when our bodies are in a position that affirms a downward, more sluggish movement of energy; the two are invariably connected. Even our language reflects this downward movement of energy. Few would feel proud to be classified as "spineless" or as having "no backbone." There are even phrases like: "Sunk in despair; weighed down; down in the dumps; she's going downhill; down and out...." They all convey the image of a person who is *anything but* sitting up straight with an alert mind.

Compare this slumped posture to standing or sitting up

straight with graceful alertness. Concentrate on taking deep, complete breaths, using the full capacity of your lungs. Remember to keep your chest uplifted and shoulders back a little, to give the lungs room to expand. Gradually fill your lungs with air, feeling the breath enter the lower, middle, then upper portions of the chest, allowing the lungs to expand fully yet comfortably. Slowly exhale completely. Now breathe naturally, or repeat the exercise for extra rejuvenation. I like to breathe deeply out-of-doors where the air is fresh and feels even more invigorating.

Our lungs are larger in the lower portion of the chest and smaller higher up in the chest. This means that plenty of toxins can be stored in the lower areas if they remain unused, as when we take high, shallow breaths.*

Women who wore corsets had the convenience of "fainting couches" where they were able to collapse whenever they couldn't get enough air. After loosening a few sections of

---

*A relaxed diaphragm, which is vital to correct posture, allows impurities to be cleansed from our lungs as we fill them with fresh air and expel it fully. This should be a daily practice for everyone. It promotes good health and increased energy. (The diaphragm is a muscular partition that divides the chest area from the abdomen and is located below the lungs from the front of the body to the spine. When the diaphragm is relaxed, it allows the lungs to expand fully during inhalation. Additionally, this diaphragm muscle massages the abdominal organs with each expansion and contraction of the lower lung. For this reason, diaphragmatic breathing is vital to our health and well-being.)

the constraining garment, a woman could recover her breath, and her senses. Why act as if we are still physically restricted if we're not? Relax, and breathe!

Oxygen revitalizes our bodies and is an excellent cure for fatigue, lethargy, or otherwise lowered or depressed levels of energy. Our oxygenated blood nourishes all the systems of the body including the organs, the nerves and functions of the brain, the muscles, the immune system, and the glandular system. The body, with an upright form and a good supply of oxygen-nourishment, is more prepared for positive action and feels awake and ready! Phrases such as "*Rise* and shine; things are *looking up*; wake *up*; what an *upstanding* individual; I feel *uplifted*; keep your *chin up*" illustrate the link between the physical upright position and mental clarity or alertness.

Good posture also promotes a feeling, both physical and mental, of being centered. In skiing, my coaches emphasized again and again the need for keeping the body's energy "in your center." To discover our centers, they had us (while standing or sitting up straight) first lean to the left, then move back to a straightened position and feel the center point, and then lean to the right and come back to the center again. They had us repeat this exercise a couple of times until we could sense our physical centers. It is an anchoring point of balance in the body that everyone has and can learn to feel.

Staying centered while skiing allows for immediate movement to the left or right and backward or forward. Then, if an arm or leg suddenly flails off to the side, it does not readily pull the entire body off center with it. It is easier to recover one's balance and continue without falling because the energy is anchored at a central point that can be reestablished quickly. Otherwise, an unexpected motion can easily cause a wipeout.

Similarly, when a person is centered in the way he stands and sits, then the outward flailings of conflicts, moods, or emergencies do not pull one "off center" as easily and it is easier to recover and respond with immediate action. The centering exercise my coaches taught me, of leaning left and back to center, then right and to an upright position again, can be practiced anywhere, both sitting and standing. When the pace of my life becomes frenzied and my energy gets "out there," I know that I'm not centered. I check my posture and focus for a few minutes on the technique of leaning from side to side. When we're centered, it allows grace to flow more freely.

Being centered is not at all the same as being controlled. Centeredness is a calm and relaxed state. It enables a person to adapt and to handle new situations without reacting out of proportion to the circumstances, both physically and mentally. A person who is controlled is tense with the inner hope or expectation that things will go according to *his* plan or idea. *When* there is a change (not if), that control is shattered and throws the person off balance almost immediately. Strict control usually leads to a sudden outburst of the repressed feelings, rather than a graceful recovery to the center of balance.

Proper posture alone will not change mental attitudes, but the increase in energy coupled with a willingness to change and the practice of positive, new ways of facing life will allow astonishing transformations to take place.

~

The Language of the Eyes

Looking people in the eyes when talking with them shows that you are consciously listening and responding. The eyes often convey our thoughts and are considered the "windows of the soul" by some. There is a whole language of the eyes. A person can communicate love, laughter, pain, sorrow, compassion, sparkling interest, and countless other feelings through the eyes. A person can say one thing using words and quite another by a look from the eyes. I have seen anger and hatred shoot from the eyes like bullets, without a word being said, and eyes that look blank and unresponsive to life around them. What we convey with our eyes does affect those around us. It is therefore beneficial to use the language of our eyes to express and transmit the energy of graciousness.

However, do keep in mind that customs vary in different countries. In some places it may be rude or have a suggestive meaning to look straight into a person's eyes. If you are a world traveler, you may want to check on local customs so that the impression you give is the one you intend.

In the American culture, eyes that look straight ahead express an alert interest or the willingness to face whatever lies ahead. Eyes that are constantly roving indicate a lack of interest (looking for something better elsewhere), restlessness, an avoidance of what they are facing, or even untruthfulness. Eyes that look downward imply a downcast or depressed energy—one of submission, fatigue, or of hiding something. But eyes calmly looking down and off to the side may indicate a posture of thoughtfulness or mulling things over. Glancing upward, when done while conversing with others, can indicate trying to see over a person to something better. When in a reflective or meditative state, looking upward is often the eyes' natural position when seeking higher guidance, inspiration, or uplifting thoughts—but it isn't very kind to imply that you can't receive uplifting thoughts from the person with whom you are speaking! Yet eyes that look upward and off to the side seem to indicate someone who is casting in thought for a new direction or solution. So, looking a person in the eyes is more than just good manners. It communicates respect to others and can say more about how you feel than the words you choose.

Express Appreciation

Saying "Please" and "Thank you" *sincerely* to others helps us to learn appreciation for all acts of kindness, gestures of respect and friendship; to express forgiveness; and to strengthen the bonds of humanity.

When we are asking a person to do something for us, it is hardly polite to demand compliance. "Give me the milk, will you?" lends a different impression than a kindly requested "Will you please pass me the milk?" We are asking a favor of the person, so it's nice to regard it as one and ask kindly.

Saying a genuine "Thank you" also dispels the tendency to take others for granted or take for granted the gifts we receive from life.

Have we adopted the attitude that this thing, and that, should be done for us? Do we expect to have everything given to us? People won't enjoy bestowing gifts or offering to do us favors if they are received as though we deserved *at least* that much, and possibly more. And if we are ungrateful long enough, we'll end up miserable with everything we have—it will never be enough.

When we return even the smallest favor with a heartfelt "Thank you," we open ourselves to allow more kindness and grace to flow into our lives.

Sit and Walk Gracefully

Sitting down or standing up from a chair with a graceful movement is also reflective of more than good etiquette. Moving the body gracefully helps the mind to feel more calm and peaceful. When the body is moving restlessly at all times, how can the mind be calm and centered? If the mind isn't calm and centered, it is hard to focus one's attention on anything. The body and mind are linked both physically and through the energy of one's thoughts. Scattered physical energy usually corresponds to scattered thoughts. Any activity that includes graceful movement also promotes calmness and graciousness in thought—even when it is how we sit down, stand up, or walk across a room.

My father's mother taught me a great deal about the link between physical movements and one's general disposition—even though I'm sure that it wasn't her intention. She was not one of those sweet, kindhearted grandmothers children adore. She was a grumpy, self-centered woman who had the sourest expression on her face that I have ever seen. I stare with near-disbelief at old photographs of her deeply frowning face, with a matching resentful look in her eyes. Her visage would probably seem adorable to me if only her personality didn't coincide. As with many people, her temperament was clearly etched in the lines and expression on her face.

In my mind the duty of a grandmother is to slightly spoil her darling little grandchildren with cookies and cake and with happy outings to the park or the nearby zoo. Well, my grandmother must never have had these things explained to her. When we went to her house for dinner, she served us plain boiled chicken and baked winter squash. There may be some people who love pale, rubbery-skinned chicken and squash with nothing on it, but we were the wrong audience for her culinary presentations (a little butter and brown sugar on the squash would have done much to improve her standing in our young eyes). These were not meals that my sister and I dreamed of—we prided ourselves on being able to actually eat them! My grandmother didn't even have packaged cookies to hand out to us after the meal. And we did feel that we deserved some type of reward for eating all the food she put on our plates.

It would have been totally understandable, and her efforts even touchingly appreciated, if she had been unable to do more, but she was just being crotchety. We seemed to bring it out in her. No trips to the park, no bouncing us on her knees, no reading to us our favorite picture-book stories on a rainy afternoon—there was no gentle, grandmotherly kindness to her! Her small meannesses only confused us. Our mother would gently take us girls aside and reassure us that it wasn't our fault that our grandmother wasn't nicer to us but that she was that way with everyone. What a sad commentary on her behavior.

Our dour grandmother also moved around as though every motion was a bother and an irritation to her. It probably was. I can picture her struggling to get up out of a chair, her little grunts and groans of dissatisfaction only adding to the image of age and unhappiness.

I vowed at an early age that I would never become like her when I grew up. Fresh-baked cookies and loving attention would be my motto for the role of grandmother.

Much to my surprise, I found years later that I was beginning (at a young age) to groan and moan when trying to get up off a sofa or rise from a chair. It's true that I was extremely sore from doing a lot of hard physical work, but there I was in my thirties, groaning like my grandmother! I couldn't believe I had let that sneak into my life.

I have to admit that it is a poor habit to form—and a habit it becomes all too easily. Leaving out those little groans and struggles can be a lot more difficult than one would think! When I have sore, strained, and overworked muscles, I wish that I could be exempt from having to gracefully and soundlessly rise from a chair—but it's only because I'm not matching my actions to my beliefs. I keep trying to maintain physical grace, though, because I've noticed that, through their body language, some people actually *look* much older than their years. Those who walk and move in a fluid, energetic manner seem more youthful than those whose movements look stiff and measured from discomfort. Graceful movements in people imply more openness and interest in life, whereas stiff movements seem to imply that life is a burden that is getting the best of them.

I've found that even though it seems like the moans help us to move through the discomfort, they actually affirm the stiffness to ourselves and to others. If the stiffness is not given that verbal attention, we can rise above the discomfort mentally. The graciousness of "not noticing" the inconvenience of our stiff and aching bodies helps our minds to not give it too much importance or identify with the condition. Mentally and verbally moaning the affirmation "I ache all the time" will not help ease the situation but will encourage its persistence.

If we allow our bodies to become progressively stiff with age or overuse, we have only ourselves to blame if we do nothing about it. Rather than allow stiff muscles to rule my actions, I decided to incorporate limbering exercises into my life. Otherwise, as the years go by, anyone's body is likely to become less flexible.

We can become physically restricted by the thoughts, "I can't do this," and, "I can't do that." Sometimes it's true, but sometimes it's just an attitude, with the body following the dictates of one's mind. I think I'll stick with my original plan of refusing to be like my grandmother...even if it hurts a little.

~

Politeness

"Be polite" is such a passive phrase for suggesting that a person consider someone other than him- or herself. And the suggestion is often met with a quick, insincere response—given more as if by rote than with heartfelt appreciation.

Politeness is meant to be more than a dispassionate "Please" or "Thank you." An insincere gesture has no meaning at all. Politeness is intended as an expression of kindness to others, where the needs and feelings of another are taken into consideration.

To a great extent, consideration for others seems to have fallen by the wayside in the quest for equal rights. A lack of consideration for others also leads to rude behavior, where one's own desires become the only thing that matters.

Rudeness has been scorned by convention because it shows total disregard for the feelings of others. A child pounding a fist on the table and screaming for attention doesn't necessarily deserve pampering and special attention. Neither does a person who rudely demands acceptance and acts without integrity. A person who behaves toward others in a demanding, insistent manner is unpleasant to be around—just like a bully.

The bully comes in all shapes, sizes, and genders. While the common expectation is of a large brute of a man with a scruffy beard, the bully can also be petite and cute—the intention to pressure or coerce others into agreement is the same. Attempting to force or manipulate people does not win friends, command respect, or gain much from life other than resentment from others. The very things a bullying person is attempting to acquire are pushed or driven away by his or her own actions.

I'm not fond of the manipulation of being a "bad person" if you don't do what someone wants, versus being "good" if you do. Nor do I like being coerced with the loss of friendship or job security as a threat.

A childhood friend I was strongly drawn to used to reject me or anyone else if we didn't comply with her wishes. She would make our lives miserable by refusing to play with, or even talk to, the unfortunate victim of her displeasure. When we did what she wanted us to do, we were her friends. If we didn't, then the privilege of friendship was at stake.

We called her Queen Bee in private, but that didn't stop any of us girls from trying to please her every whim. She was magnetic, energetic, mischievous, intelligent, delightful and good-hearted (much of the time), and a whole lot of fun. But she could manipulate like a pro.

One day, I was deeply hurt by her behavior and became fed up with her "game." I ignored her more strongly than she did me. Her silence and snubs caused no visible effect. This surprised her. We went to the same elementary school, lived on the same block, and had the same friends. But I "didn't notice her" when I walked to school or was in the playground at recess. Nor did I try to regain my position as her friend. If she was with one of our mutual playmates, I went to be with someone else. A couple weeks after this stalemate began, I was walking home past her house and she called out the window to me in her sweet voice and said, "Nancy, why haven't you been talking to me? Is something wrong? I'm sorry if I upset you about anything." I forgave her right away, even though I did feel cautious about entering back into her fold. But I really *did* want her to be my friend—I just wanted her to treat me more respectfully.

Her bullying tactics came to a close. As far as I can remember, she never tried the cold-shoulder bit on me again or used her friendship as a ploy to get her way. And we remained true friends long thereafter.

A person who is habitually inconsiderate of others is often surprised that he has few (if any) real friends or allies. If a person takes no one else into consideration (for other than personal gain), it is little wonder that other people tend to respond accordingly.

Being polite and kind to others draws kindness and consideration in return. Isn't that something we *all* want?

Politeness can be extended to everyone.

"After You!"

One confusing area of polite behavior nowadays is around the question of when we should offer to have someone precede us through a doorway. Why not hold the door open for a man or woman, adult or child? We don't have to follow a rigid code of behavior that a young woman holds a door open for someone older and men always hold doors for women.

There are various hierarchies involved with business relationships, men and women, a person's social standing, and a person's physical capabilities. Some are based on formal etiquette, but other situations are less exacting.

The gracious gesture of inviting someone to "please go ahead" is simply a display of respect. It is not something a man must do because a woman is so frail that it would tax her beyond her capacity to wait or hold a door. Men know better than that by now! But they should also know to respect women and express it through their manners.

There are a few guidelines that will work in most situations. If a person is elderly, offer to have them precede you. If it is an elderly gentleman who then offers to hold the door for you to go ahead of him, accept the gesture graciously. A gentleman of any age should still show courtesy toward a woman and offer to have her precede him. A woman doesn't have to comply if she doesn't care to and can even join him at the door and hold it for him in turn. That's her choice. But it is then best to, at the very least, be polite in refusing his gesture.

A pregnant woman, too, could be encouraged to go ahead—but don't say, "Oh, I see that you're pregnant; please go ahead." She may not be pregnant, just rounded in her figure. Make your offer but leave out the comment about her forth-coming child. If a person is in a wheelchair, he is probably experienced enough with it to know how to get through doors without help, but treat handicapped persons with the same politeness you would anyone else and hold the door with respect—not pity. They will let you know if they prefer to manage the doorway on their own. Also, a person who has his hands full with children, bags, or other encumbrances should be offered the opportunity to get to his destination with as much ease as possible.

The main point is that politeness takes the other person into account. Whoever gets to a door first can most easily offer to hold it open for the next person who comes along. If the person about to pass through the doorway prefers to manage the door alone, it is polite to allow that freedom of choice.

There are some situations that differ because of the terrain. If exiting a bus, train, or walking anywhere the steps or going is difficult, it is more polite for the man, or more able-bodied person, to go first in case the other person needs assistance. This usually applies when two people are traveling together, but you can always offer your assistance if someone you don't know looks as though they are in need. But this doesn't mean we have to wait at the foot of the steps to help everyone exit safely. It also does not imply that if we are traveling alone, it is polite to barge ahead of others or nudge them out of our way!

How Fast Are We Going?

Sometimes it can be very difficult to keep pace with other people as they walk. They either stride along like they're in some kind of a race or move so slowly that they may be left behind.

It's a nice gesture to set your stride to match the person you are accompanying. It may take self-discipline and patience to adjust to someone who moves very slowly, but it is the only respectful thing you can do. Impatiently telling them to hurry up is not very gracious or polite.

It is also difficult if you end up having to practically sprint to keep up with your companion. It is fine to politely ask that person if he would mind slowing down. I don't object to asking a person several times if he would walk more slowly, if he has inadvertently sped up again. But if a speedy companion doesn't change the pace, you will either have to resign yourself to some aerobic walking exercise or show up at the destination after your friend. If it is a chronic habit, try to walk with someone else in the future.

This brings to mind another matter concerning speed—driving. If the person who is riding in your vehicle is clutching the seat or handhold with an anxious expression or words of dismay, then you are making them feel uncomfortable. If your passenger asks you to slow down, don't argue with him! Slow down. He needs to feel safe with you, even if it means you are creeping along. Choose streets where this won't matter, and enjoy looking at all the things you normally don't have time to notice. Also, you shouldn't feel as though you need to speed up to accommodate your passenger's impatience. Driving safely is more important.

My most notable first date with a young man was when I was in my late teens. My date showed up in a Porsche, and within three blocks of my home in a quiet residential neighborhood, he was passing a car on a straightaway at 60 miles an hour. Another automobile was approaching us in the other lane, so what did he do? He drove *to the left* of the approaching car and up the curb onto the grass-covered parking strip on the opposite side of the street from where we belonged. He passed both vehicles with a calm flick of the steering wheel and went back into the original lane. My first word of the evening was four letters long—I forgot my manners.

Privacy

People need privacy, especially those who lead very public lives. Intrusions at all hours and all places is not appropriate, even amongst friends. A brief smile or a few words of greeting may be all the contact a person is wanting to accept at the moment.

Restaurants are public places, but it doesn't mean that anyone dining out wants to interact with all the patrons and passersby. People need to eat somewhere, but when they are seated alone, with another person, or in a group, that is the equivalent of their own dining room table. You may greet them cordially as you pass or nod to them from a distance. If you do address a friend at a table, then also acknowledge anyone else present whose attention is turned toward you. And when you depart, after saying your farewells to your friend, at least nod and smile to the others present as you leave to acknowledge that you interrupted their time—even if it was by their request. Do not invite yourself to dinner (or breakfast), or impose yourself. It's the same as crashing someone's party, which cannot be considered polite under any circumstances.

Leave others to their conversation, and keep your attention on your own table and its occupants. People other than those you arranged to meet are not there to entertain you, nor are they obligated to in any way. If any friends you encounter act somewhat formal, distant, or awkward, then take that as your hint. If your presence is welcome, then you will be invited to join them. It is not a slight if you are not included, unless they intentionally make it one. Visit with the person another time when you can converse more comfortably.

A close friend was dining out with someone she had not seen in a long time. When they were seated, it was right next to a woman that her gentleman-friend worked with and had known for years. The woman was having dinner with her father. The tables were 2 feet apart, and there was no possibility of either couple having a private conversation. It was slightly awkward after the introductions and opening comments were made, until my friend's companion handled the matter perfectly by saying, "We'll take a table in the other room to allow you two time alone to talk." This took the privacy of both parties into account and the waitress saw to it that my friend and her partner were re-seated. Everyone had a lovely evening, with friendly nods of farewell as the first pair left the restaurant.

~

Phone Calls

Phone calls are wonderful to receive—at certain times. I considered the phone call from an acquaintance (not a close friend, who would have known better!) at 6:30 A.M. on Easter Sunday to be outrageously ill-mannered conduct. It was made more unbelievable because she was calling to ask a favor! The shock factor was so great that she received a stunned "Yes." The acquaintance hung up after a quick, "Thanks! See you soon," as part of the favor entailed me getting out of bed to do her bidding. But I was awake by then, so why not? Even though she got the results she wanted, she did *not* gain a friend.

Anything short of "Your house is on fire!" or an equivalent emergency can wait for a more reasonable hour.

If you know a person well, there is leeway in when you can call them—as long as they have told you that it is fine to call up to such-and-such a time. Otherwise, a good rule for polite phoning is to wait until 9:00 A.M. on weekdays, a bit later on Saturdays, and after 10:00 A.M. on Sundays. Some people like to sleep in on weekends.

Evening phone calls should not be placed when a person is likely to be preparing dinner. And 8:00 P.M. is a nice cutoff time, unless you are sure that calling up until 9:00 is fine.

If I know someone well, I don't mind a call a little later in the evening. This person knows my schedule and knows when I'm likely to be free to chat. But if it is only a casual acquaintance or a stranger, I don't want to hear from them late at night, nor do I want to interrupt my dinner preparations to talk. Evenings are a time when many people unwind from the activities of the day, and their desire for relaxation should be honored.

Whatever time of day or night you are calling, ask if it is a good time for that person to talk. Is she free right now, or would later be better? This is a delightfully considerate gesture, and one that is appreciated by people who have a schedule to keep or are too busy for more than the briefest conversation.

It allows the person who is receiving a call to have a choice in the matter. She has the option to respond, "I only have a couple minutes." And if she specifies a length of time, then watch the clock, and be respectful enough to stick to her time line. If she says, "Now is fine," then take her at her word. Show respect to the people you are calling—their lives do not revolve around your schedule.

"May I Help?"

If a person drops something, do you pick it up for him? Sometimes. When my large bag of groceries split open in the supermarket parking lot, and oranges, lemons, containers of milk and juice, vegetables, and more were rolling down the slope toward the storefront and lodging under parked cars, I was happy to have a stranger offer to help me pick things up.

It is polite to offer your assistance saying, "I'll get that for you," or, "Would you like some help?" And allow the person time to say either, "Oh, thank you," or, "Please don't bother." You will have to be sensitive to the situation. If he says, "Don't bother," he may mean that he doesn't want you to or that he is afraid of inconveniencing you. If he says, "Don't help," then honor his refusal politely, or, if you honestly feel that he may not be completely sincere with his "no," then offer a second time by saying, "I don't mind." Then the formalities are over. Follow the other person's wishes. If he still says no, then move on. He may have personal reasons for wanting to pick up his own things.

We often fall short of having perfect interactions with others. We may reflect after an encounter that we didn't handle it very well, but we have to allow ourselves mistakes and try to correct them next time.

Simply speaking, if you know a person doesn't want you to do something, then don't. But if this person appreciates your words and gestures that express your sensitivity, thoughtfulness, and esteem for him, then you will experience a wonderful exchange of giving and receiving pleasantries with one another. That is the real beauty behind the social graces. It is like a rhythmic dance of kindness, appreciation, and respect. It's nicer to dance through life than battle one's way.

Learning to Listen to Life

Listening to, and not interrupting, others is an element of grace. It teaches us to value others and to respect them as having equal merit in the larger scheme of life. Listening carelessly to the words of others can become an insidious habit. Life starts passing us by unnoticed if our time is spent anxiously awaiting a chance to voice our own opinion as though it is the only important one. We have to be alert to learn this difficult lesson—our own swirling thoughts, ideas, and preoccupations can all too easily cloud our ability to listen carefully and attentively to other people. In the fast-paced world we live in, it is harder to slow down enough to hear what is really going on around us, but it is still as essential as ever.

Grace comes from knowing how to *listen* to another person—not to sit quietly and tune him out due to boredom or impatience, but (sitting or standing up straight!) to listen with attention. It pays to listen carefully lest you miss hearing something of importance—even, or I should say especially, when it is from someone you think has nothing important to say. That is often where we can learn the most—if we don't discover words of wisdom, then we might at least learn about our own impatience concerning another person's views.

~

Learning Grace

Drawing grace into our lives *is* a skill that can be learned. Some people are more naturally inclined to be graceful or gracious, but if there is a sincere interest, anyone can make grace a part of his life. If we want something, it requires self-effort to get it. We want a new job? It won't come to us unless we apply for one or accept an opportunity that presents itself. When we need to go somewhere, we find a mode of transportation. If we need new clothing, we have to shop for it—it won't appear suddenly on our doorsteps. And if want grace, we need to seek it and be open to receiving it in our lives.

Once the fundamentals are brought into practice, they can be honed and refined through each situation. I wish it were a simple matter of learning how to do something, then knowing how to repeat it the remainder of one's life. But it's not that straightforward for anyone. Each situation, and every environment, requires a fresh approach to grace—although the principles remain the same.

Expressing grace—in business, in the home, at school, with

friends and strangers—will always bring new challenges. It's astonishing how many provocations the universe can create for us. An all-new or even a recurring incitement will inevitably strike the moment you think that you have a handle on acting with grace. Then, all of a sudden, you'll find yourself facing a challenge again. The dramatic shift from being centered, and in harmony with the universe, to a great test in acting with grace can happen very swiftly. But it makes life more exciting this way.

In striving to develop grace in your life, there will be moments when you reach a personal victory in an area where you have been struggling—small triumphs that may go unnoticed by others yet mark the beginning of a new way of being. There will also be moments of temporary lapses into old, unwanted habits, which may be firmly rooted in a pattern of behavior. But with a steady willingness to change and deep concentration on new ways to think or act, we can, often quite suddenly, find that old habits have greatly diminished or even vanished forever. The concentrated power of thought is a tremendous force and can change one's patterns of behavior, even overnight.

Does Acting with Grace Guarantee Happiness?

Not every situation has a built-in triumphant success. The success may be that you have done your best to act with honesty and integrity, yet the situation will not be a happy one no matter how well you behave. We can't control the behavior of others, and we don't have complete control over any particular situation. There is an energy greater than ourselves that is always the unseen factor.

However, defeat can end up, in reality, to be the success, bringing a new direction or outlook. On the other hand, a seeming success can end up being a person's downfall, triggering qualities and patterns of behavior that destroy, rather than build, a person's character. Since we can't foresee the future, it's important just to do the best we can in each situation, learn from it, and then go forward. In this way, an attunement with the universal flow of grace can be established and flourish.

There is an inner awareness of grace when one has acted thoughtfully, been calmly centered, listened to the other person's point of view, and acted in a respectful manner. Grace or graciousness in any situation allows for the differences in people's outlooks and doesn't attempt to *force* everyone into agreement. This is a sign of an attunement to a greater reality than our own individual lives.

Voicing an Opinion, or Demanding Agreement?

Prior to the 1920s, American women simply didn't voice their own opinions in public. Instead, a woman was guided by her husband's or parents' opinions, and that was thought to be good enough. That was before women could vote. Now things have changed.

There have been few social guidelines on how to voice an opinion considerately. It seems that no one wanted to encourage the voicing of opinions other than his own. Now that women can "have their say" in any matter, it only reinforces the importance of "saying" it graciously.

Difficulty can arise, however, when others do not agree with our opinions and especially when they voice their disagreement loudly and disrespectfully. It's hard to respond considerately when little consideration is given in return. Each person's opinion is as valid as another's—no matter whose is more carefully thought out. But people have an equal right to disagree—and they surely will on some things. It becomes even more awkward when a woman's opinion is based on her feelings, and the other opinion (a man's possibly?) is based solely on logic. This can easily lead to a stalemate. So how can we get others to respect our opinions?

The elements of grace—being centered, calm, respectful, and listening carefully to the other person—will help tremendously. Being gracious in all situations shows wisdom, inner strength, and courage.

Truth is more important than mere agreement. Seek the truth of a situation, even if others don't see it the way you do. It takes maturity to give consideration to another person's views, and not everyone will have that maturity.

Harsh words, a shrill voice, and a belittling attitude will only show to others an inner restlessness, conflict, and insecurity. A demanding voice will tend to bring rejection, no matter the wisdom of the words. By your reactions to any disagreement, you can help magnetize increasingly more respect, *or* disrespect.

Women seem to be more aware of their inner power or strength when expressing themselves with feeling, which comes from the center of their feminine natures. Yet the tone of voice, as well as the words chosen, should convey sincere respect, indicating that the other person's views have been heard. Men especially don't usually respond well to a woman whose voice reflects emotion. They may even stop listening to what a woman is saying if her tone of voice shifts to express her feelings. The more emotion and frustration a woman expresses (because she is being ignored or disagreed with), the less she is likely to be heard respectfully.

A woman friend of mine told me that she is always careful to leave any hint of emotion out of her voice whenever she is attending a meeting that includes men. She has repeatedly noticed that men seem to instantly lose respect for a woman as soon as she comes forth with an emotionally charged opinion. A woman who conveys her feelings through her tone of voice implies that she is trying to sway the other person or people to her own view, heedless of their opinions—and people don't like that.

Other people will best hear and respect a person's opinion if it is stated calmly, clearly, and with deep conviction. A willingness to reassess honestly or test the validity of one's own opinions will also help gain respect and agreement from others. And finally, showing sincere respect for the opinions of others will magnetize a mutual appreciation.

~

Our Opinions on a Better Way of Life

Our opinions on general issues are one area where we tend to be adamant in our views. The awakening of enthusiasm and awareness of "new and greater things" is another.

When awareness of new and greater things arises, beware of the tendency toward a fanatical view. With the excess zeal of new discoveries, our thoughts and energies often zoom off in the new direction and toss the concept of balance into the ether—this "thing" or way of being is *it*! And not only is this the answer for you—it's the answer for everyone! What other way of life could there be? All these other people, poor things, are missing out.

It's natural to want to share one's enthusiasm, but—what a surprise!—not everyone else is interested.

You may experience a vast improvement in your health by changing the types of food you eat or discover a fabulous and easy way to lose weight. Will everyone you meet want to try it? No. It doesn't matter if the results of this great new thing are plain for everyone to see. They may not want to hear about it, let alone try it themselves. If a person doesn't seem intrigued with your idea or findings within a couple minutes, then change the topic and talk about something else. You can make an abrupt shift by interjecting something like, "Oh well, I could go on and on about that. Tell me, how is your..." and act interested.

Be centered, even if enthusiastically, when sharing your new idea or discovery. Then you won't be so let down if it's not met with an equal response. People will hear and understand it, in time, if it truly resonates with them.

~

Tension and Stress

When a person is said to be uptight, few, if any, would consider this a compliment or a desirable state. Tension, once allowed free rein, is triggered more and more frequently with alarmingly little provocation. It is the root of much disharmony—physical, mental, and emotional.

A person's physical movements can be greatly impaired by tense muscles, which cause pain and discomfort. Physical tension can be from tired, overworked muscles or the result of mental tension and stress transferred to the body. Whatever its source, tension blocks energy. It also creates disturbances in the basic functions of the body—digestive and circulatory problems included.

Mental tension can cause a narrowing of one's thoughts and mental outlook. If an individual is acting uptight, other people instinctively try to avoid the negative energy that person is spewing forth. Everyone must know someone who, when tense and uptight, can fill a room with his negativity without even saying a word. People tiptoe around him to avoid confrontation and flee the scene as quickly as possible. Negativity is a powerful force to be reckoned with. That uptight individual will not be pleasantly receptive to solutions or new ideas. Tension tends to create negative emotional responses—not an open, willing attitude.

Tension can be eased from our lives when we act in accordance with the balanced principles of grace. Through self-awareness, and an expanded view of life, tension and stress can be recognized and released before they explode into a harmful, destructive force.

A gracious outlook reduces or dispels the small irritations and problems that can enter and disrupt the harmony of our lives. Eliminating them provides an opening for a positive attitude that looks immediately to ways to solve or harmonize a difficult situation. Tension locks energy into a static condition, but once the tense response is eliminated, we free the energy in our bodies. And we can also stop locking it in our thoughts, where negative reactions can churn for years without finding resolution and peace.

Here are a few tension-relieving exercises that can be done anytime you need a little relief—even at the office. These are all easy, gentle movements, but as is true with all exercises, only do that which is comfortable for your body. In all three exercises, breathing should be done through the nostrils with both the inhalation and exhalation.

1. This first exercise is done while sitting in a chair. Start by sitting up straight, with your hands in your lap. Gracefully raise your arms over your head and reach up with your fingertips so they reach above your shoulders. Inhale. Then exhale as you lower your arms close to your body in front of you in a

calm motion. Begin to bend forward at the waist and have your hands travel down along the sides of your calves as you continue bending forward until your head reaches your knees and your arms hang loosely at your sides, and expel the last of your breath.

Now, breathe naturally as you concentrate on relaxing the lower back, the neck and shoulders, the arms and hands, the legs and feet. You may like the image of breathing in space as you inhale gently, calmly exhaling tensions. Remain in this relaxed position for a few moments. Then, while inhaling slowly, draw your hands up your calves and close to your body as you rise into an upright sitting position (use your hands on your legs or knees to relieve strain to your lower back if you feel any discomfort there). Then, once you are sitting up straight, continue in one fluid motion to raise your hands high above your head, giving a slight stretch at the top. End with relaxing your arms back down in front of your chest into your lap, with your palms up. Take a few full, deep breaths to complete the relaxation and feel bathed in calmness.

2. This next pose gives a slight twist to the upper body and helps relax the abdomen, chest, back, neck, and shoulders. It should be done slowly and gently. The goal is not to get into a particular position but to relax.

Sit up straight in a chair, with your palms facing upward in your lap. Now place your *right* hand on the outside of your *left* knee or thigh, depending on your flexibility, and then your *left* hand on the side or back of your chair. Keep your abdomen relaxed as you inhale and gently straighten your spine.

Relax your neck—rather than twisting it for you to face a certain way.

As you calmly exhale, gently twist your body farther toward your *left* hand on the back of the chair. Keep your neck, back, and chest relaxed. Take a few deep breaths in this position and concentrate on relaxing your upper body. Then, to come out of the pose, inhale deeply one more time, return to the initial straightened position with your hands still on your leg and back of the chair. Exhale and gracefully release your hands and face forward with both hands in your lap, palms up.

Rest for a moment, then proceed with a twist to the other side and repeat the pose as described above but with your *right* leg and *left* hand this time.

3. The last exercise is for a total relaxation and consists of deep, diaphragmatic breathing. Wear clothing that is loose around your waist and remove your belt if you're wearing one. For an even more soothing effect, play music that promotes relaxation. I recommend not trying this pose at the office, as your co-workers may find you half-asleep on the floor.

Most of us do not expel all the air from our lungs, nor consciously fill them completely as we breathe. In this position, there is nothing to restrict the flow.

Lie down on your back on a mat or rug on the floor. Place your hands on your abdomen at and above your navel and try to relax your whole body. Especially make sure that your abdomen is relaxed.

Begin by calmly exhaling through the nose any air remaining in your lungs and notice how your hands lower with your abdomen as you exhale fully. Now inhale through the nostrils in a deep, slow, soothing breath using your diaphragm and mentally observe your hands rising as air fills the lower part of the lungs. Feel the air expanding the rib cage as it rises up into the middle then upper regions of the chest.

Pause for a few moments without straining, then exhale slowly while relaxing your body more deeply as the air gradually flows out, using the diaphragm to expel the last of the air. Repeat. Relax your entire body with each breath. Close your eyes while practicing this exercise to help you focus on the sense of peace filling your body. Continue this practice for several minutes.

Every adult is familiar with stress in some form. Stress can create a great amount of tension if we don't learn how to release it or channel it into a positive direction. Some people are excellent at handling stress in a productive way, but it does take practice.

I have had frequent occasions to cater as well as hostess parties. Cooking a meal for 35 people is not unusual for such events, and I have had to learn how to cope with the accompanying stress.

It is natural for anyone to get tense over all the details involved with entertaining guests: Is the table set? Are the flowers arranged and new candles in the holders? Did the silver get polished? Are the windows clean? Oh no!—I didn't get enough asparagus or onions or whipping cream…And then, if not extremely well-organized, it is easy to get behind schedule. Quick, get the salad made—and where's the salad dressing?

Where are the serving bowls? Are the water glasses filled yet? The hostess wants everything to turn out perfectly and tensions can build easily.

There were times when I was late getting things ready and would end up literally running down the hallway in order to quickly change my clothes in time for the arriving guests. But after that, just as quickly, I had to be as calm, centered, and as relaxed as possible.

What has the most importance? Who wants a tense or exhausted hostess? And who wants to eat a meal cooked with an attitude of tension or resentment rather than as a loving offering to the guests? The goal is to have your guests relax and have an enjoyable time. If the hostess is uptight about all the details, how can the guests relax and enjoy the gathering? The details have importance on one level, but in the broader perspective, the guests will have a better time if the hostess is gracious and at ease than if the silver is polished.

If stress is allowed to build as tension, illness or disharmony will eventually occur. The vital point in handling this kind of stress is to keep the energy moving and not let it stop and store in the body as tension. For this reason, many people are turning to activities such as yoga postures, tai chi, workout programs, jogging, team sports, and various other avenues for channeling energy into positive action. Yoga postures and other practices that focus on calming the body and mind and gracefully stretching to release stored physical and mental tensions are becoming especially popular.

Whatever method is practiced, those that help on the

deepest levels work on releasing the pent-up energy in an affirmative direction rather than through expressing anger, hatred, resentment, or other display of disharmony.

~

How to Cope with Fear

Fear can block or "freeze" energy. I think that everyone must know that experience of being frozen, or paralyzed, by fear or panic. A person "cowers in fear," or in the opposite condition, "exudes confidence" or "bristles with energy." The fearful, cowering pose illustrates someone who has allowed fear to block the use of his energy until there isn't even enough energy available to hold the body upright! Yet those who exude confidence and bristle with energy have so much energy coursing through them that it becomes nearly tangible—they couldn't cower if they wanted to!

Once energy is increased—which is what a boost of adrenalin does in the body's natural reaction to an emergency—it helps a person handle a situation he would normally find difficult, if not impossible.

The Fears Encountered in Daily Life

There are various fears that can prevent us from facing elements of our daily lives. Learning ways to increase consciously the body's available energy helps anyone cope with feeling fearful or insecure.

People have problems facing all kinds of commonplace

things—handling financial matters, entering into a new job or social situation, meeting new people, speaking in front of a group, visiting the dentist or doctor, entertaining an important or influential person, learning a new skill, dealing with emotional issues—the list goes on. Even social interactions that are awkward for one's own particular social type can produce a kind of fear.

To combat a fear or insecurity, adhere to the outward postures of grace: Check your posture, and make yourself stand, or sit, up straight. Keep your chin up and level; meet the person (or situation) by calmly looking straight at him (or it). Make sure that you are breathing deeply, not shallowly, so you can draw plenty of oxygen into your body. Listen rather than let yourself start talking uncontrollably. Try to be aware of your "center," and relax any tension buildup that could be pulling you away from that point of balance. Get your mind to help you—mentally tell yourself that you need more energy to face this person (or situation) and regard yourself with dignity and respect. Keep your thoughts as positive as possible so that even in an unpleasant encounter you can maintain your calmness and dignity.

Emergency or Crisis Situations

There are times when a crisis strikes. How can the concept of grace apply in an emergency? Emergencies require more than merely standing up straight and taking a few deep breaths. An emergency often entails controlling fear while a solution is sought or action is being taken.

One example is when a child has an accident and hurts himself severely. The child looks to his mother, father, or other more mature person for comfort and reassurance. It is not the time to show a reaction of fear or anxiety. It will only scare the child and amplify the child's distress.

Communicating fear can actually immobilize one's ability to handle a situation. If trepidation is allowed to magnify into hysterics, there is little chance of functioning productively. Additionally, overt panic is contagious and can make a crisis situation much worse for the others involved. An emergency is best handled as calmly and quickly as possible. The needs of others have absolute priority. One's own feelings just don't matter.

When I was active in the local volunteer fire department, we were often called out on medical emergencies and accidents. It was essential to our job to keep the people involved in the incident as calm as possible. If they were wildly agitated, we couldn't get close enough to aid them. We had to be composed and try to tangibly extend our calmness to them.

When there was an unpleasant condition, I would block any emotions that interfered with my ability to handle the situation and wait until later to release my feelings.

Delayed reaction is common with people who face an emergency. Yet as many people have come to learn, it isn't good to stuff the feeling of fear, where it can harbor in the body or mind. However, it *can* be set aside temporarily. A person can always handle it later, after the ordeal, to ease the stress from a situation and express (even privately, just to oneself) what it was *really* like.

Fear is a state where our attention and energy are focused inwardly—contracting in toward ourselves, "What might happen to me?" or, "What might happen to this person (or thing) that I love?" The thought of self allows fear to take hold.

Giving to others (or to a situation) in an outward way keeps the energy moving through and away from yourself. Your thought and concern for others sets your own needs aside, and fear is placed in abeyance. Giving energy, particularly with love, is a powerful force.

Love is a great antidote for combating fear. Put yourself into a mode of giving loving energy. If you can't feel love, try giving compassion or another heartfelt quality. The act of giving loving energy helps disperse any fear, even the instinctive, panic-inducing kind. You can use mental imagery to help learn how to face an ordeal in a loving way. Rather than shrink back from fear, you can learn to counteract it with positive energy and actions.

Instinctive Fears

A panicked reaction is always a bit embarrassing because we seem to "lose it" in these situations. But some things just push us past our point of being able to control our reactions or feelings. The panic can be triggered by a fear of mice, snakes, spiders, heights, confined spaces, and so on. It can also occur in interactions with people or in people-oriented situations. With these instinctive fears, grace is the last thing on a person's mind. We react like it is a life-threatening situation, even when it isn't.

All you can do in a panic situation is regain your composure as quickly as possible. Use the same guidelines that help you face the known or expected insecurities. Take full, deep breaths; stand or sit up straight to give yourself access to physical and emotional stores of energy; and if you are with someone, tell them that you have to get away from whatever it is right away. Sometimes a person who knows of your fear can help you calm down and get through it.

There are a couple of things that trigger my fears, and no, I'm not telling. That is one of my tricks. I try to get through my fears as though they do not have a strong hold, with the awareness that they *can* go away. If we don't give energy that reinforces something, then it will weaken and change.

However, one day, I was hit with a double whammy. I was starting to freeze up with fear as I was coping for a long period of time with one of my nemeses. I told my husband, Kerry, that I didn't think that I could go ahead, and he took my hand and told me that he would help me, and that I would be fine—and I was. I was quite proud of myself. But within three minutes, I was faced with another big fear. I bolted after 10 seconds at a quick sprint. Two fears in a row was too many.

A friend who was with us turned to Kerry and asked, "What's wrong with Nancy?" Kerry played it down and soon joined me where I was sitting and recovering from the incidents. It had been years since I had experienced either of those fears. I sat up straight (rather than holding my head in my hands and cowering), breathed deeply, and pictured calming energy pouring into my body at the medulla oblongata (the hollow spot at the base of the skull), filling every body cell with peace and harmony. I then visualized it spreading out toward others through the area of my heart. It was the only way I could give heartfelt energy under the circumstances, as I knew no one around me.*

When our friend joined us a few minutes later, I was able to go on as though all was well. It was. I knew that the fear was not based on present circumstances but was simply an instinctive reaction that I have. I treat the situations as impersonally as possible and then go on.

By developing the art of responding to fear with a conscious increase in energy and centeredness and giving that to others, uncontrollable fears can be lessened so that you will be able to gracefully, if swiftly, walk away from their source.

With conscientious practice, grace will develop a stronger influence in your life. In time, it will reduce the impact of larger tests that will surely come your way.

Whatever level of fear you must face, manage it by filling yourself with the energy of grace. It will help you to breeze through situations that you once believed to be monumental.

---

*According to the ancient science of yoga, energy enters the body at the medulla oblongata. In Western medicine, it is known as a key component to the automatic systems of the body, such as the heart rate, respiration, blood pressure, and the body's temperature. It is the communication center through which the sensory and motor nerves relay information to and from the brain to the rest of the body.

Worry and Anxiety

Worry and anxiety are forms of fear where there is still energy but it is out of balance or scattered. It's a bit like a washing machine that is going off balance—it wobbles out of its normal smoothly spinning pattern until it is thrown so far off balance that it comes to a halt. Worries and anxieties, if allowed to continue unchecked, can also bring us to a halt—by rendering us incapable of making a decision or unable to act in a situation out of fear of doing the wrong thing.

In milder forms, worry and anxiety can be ever-present in the background of our lives: Are the children going to be late for school? Where are the car keys? I forgot to call about canceling my appointment—I hope it's not too late! These milder forms can be dispersed just by taking a few deep breaths and giving yourself a moment to pause and recenter yourself.

Some days, though, the near-constant addition of more and more things that need to be done augments worry or anxiety right along with the increasing number of duties or projects that provoke these feelings.

Worry and anxiety interfere with our abilities to handle situations comfortably. They hinder clarity of thought, fluidity of movement, and ease in adapting to new situations, and they usually affect our equanimity. Then, our emotional state becomes overly sensitive from the agitated, uneven flow of energy. Worry and anxiety are merely variations of fear—based on the thought that something is going to go wrong or not work out as you hope or cannot be accomplished in time.

The same principles of increased energy to help us face fear will also help to smooth out and balance our scattered energies from worry and anxiety. By catching apprehension and uneasiness in their early stages and restoring balance or harmony, the source of the concerns can be dealt with more directly, more quickly, and more competently.

Are We Working with Mind, Matter, or Both?

The mind is a tricky thing, and unless we guide our thoughts in a positive way, they don't always work to our advantage. The social displays of grace are helpful reminders because they keep our focus on our own behaviors more than on the actions of others. They teach us how to take responsibility for the things we can control—ourselves—and to let go of the things that are beyond our power to change—the behavior of others and outer circumstances. Grace shows us how to move and act in such a way that we become calmer, more focused, and more receptive to learning from life. And it is based on respect shown toward all people.

You will discover a surprising benefit from incorporating this approach of grace into your life. But remember that the physical acts are merely social pretenses unless there is an internal accord. An attitude of graciousness is essential for any physical form of grace to flourish.

Our happiness in life stems from an attunement with any aspect of grace that is expanded to incorporate our physical actions, mental attitudes, and emotions or feelings into mutual harmony. Our inner selves can evolve and become expressed in our own unique ways through every word, gesture, and deed.

- Politeness is an expression of kindness toward others, where the needs and feelings of all whom we encounter are taken into consideration.
- The most we can do in any given situation is to act with honesty and integrity, do the best we can, and then, no matter what the outcome, go forward with life.
- A gracious outlook reduces or dispels the small tensions and problems that can enter and disrupt the harmony of our lives.
- Feelings of fear, insecurity, worry, and anxiety can be diminished, or dispelled by utilizing the outward forms of grace.

CHAPTER 5

~

Relationships

uch of our happiness and unhappiness stems from our relationships, whether or not we feel accepted or loved. We all want to be reassured that we truly are a friend, a loved one, and a desirable person to be around.

Who hasn't been disappointed in love or been hurt because of a relationship? Learning through pain is never the most pleasant way of gaining insight—even though that's often how we learn the most important lessons and meet our greatest changes. Yet it is much more gratifying and less emotionally wearing to improve our relationships voluntarily.

So, how do we build happiness into our relationships and our lives? We learn ways to improve our interactions with other people and all of life. And we develop and maintain our attunement with grace through our own behaviors.

Once we can look back at our past and say, "I've become

a kinder, more respectful, more understanding, more loving person than I used to be," then we will realize an inner happiness and growth that opens the door to ever-more fulfilling relationships. We will be on the path of grace.

The Importance of Relationships

Why do relationships matter so much? Because all of life is about how we relate to others, to ourselves, and to all of creation.

Deep love for life and for people can only be experienced by those with an open heart. To experience love, we need to allow our feelings to expand beyond our own lives to touch the lives of others or, to an even greater extent, to the essence and source of life itself.

All relationships require continuous nurturing for them to evolve and to bring out the best in everyone. We may not see some friends for extended periods at a time, but when we meet them again, a loving contact can keep the relationship deep and meaningful.

Yet one person alone cannot create a perfect relationship—it requires the cooperation and willingness of both people involved. Sadly, friends and companions may end up parting ways during the course of their lives. Rather than depend on other people for our happiness, we need to cultivate our own inner joy by embracing a positive look at life.

~

Be a True Friend to All

Friendship ought to be the foundation of *all* relationships. The outward form they take doesn't matter—our connections with nature, animals, or other people are all important. But the person we become through our relationships *does* matter. We should ask ourselves: How do I relate to life and to those around me? Do I like what I see about myself? Would I like others to treat me the same way I treat them? And if not, what would I change?

When we are willing to take responsibility for our own behaviors, we gain the ability to change what we don't like and to add qualities that will improve our lives. Practicing friendship is also a wonderful way to work with our own natures. We need to be best friends with ourselves so we can accept our own imperfections, past mistakes, or regretted actions. We need to develop *self*-kindness along with kindness toward others.

Self-Forgiveness to Forgive Others

It is easy to become caught in feeling guilty about our past actions. We all have memories of things we wish had been different—times when we said hurtful words; didn't stand by a friend or family member when we should have; were unaware of how to express our love clearly and therefore neglected to, or didn't realize how deeply we cared about someone or something until it was too late; ignored a situation that had more importance than we realized; failed at something where we had pinned high hopes; or made a decision that we now feel was wrong. Our feelings of regret and remorse can be overwhelming at times and we all experience them.

How can we forgive ourselves for past conduct or deeds? One way is to view our own lives compassionately as though they belong to someone else whom we love dearly. We make most of our errors in behavior because we don't know better at the time or are unaware of the potential repercussions. It is helpful to identify the essence of the mistake.

Ask yourself:

1. Did I know better at the time but acted compulsively anyway? Or did I just not realize that I should behave any differently?
2. Did I take the other person's feelings into consideration? Or were that person's feelings ignored because I had my own desires or ideas that overrode my normally considerate behavior?
3. Did it seem like the right thing to do at the time? Was I aware of a better alternative?
4. Was it a general miscommunication? Was the other person involved also at error?

Then, answer or counsel yourself kindly and with compassion as though talking to a friend or loved one who is telling you about his past pain or distress. Remember that the past can't be changed, but attempts can be made to change potentially regrettable behavior in the present and future, which is where solutions reside. Ease your discomfort with the following thoughts.

1(a). Well, you knew better, but it's hard to overcome habits around the way you react to others and difficult situations. Is there a way to change the outcome now? If so, then go back and fix things. If not, let it go and try not to repeat the mistake. Mentally offer the misdeed into the vast consciousness and energy of the universe, and vow that you will try your best to not make such an error again.

1(b). You didn't know better. No one had taught you to behave otherwise. You can't expect that you'll do everything just right—no one does. And you've remembered the incident and have tried to change since then.

2. You weren't as considerate as you could have been, but we all tend to get caught up in our own lives and forget to think about other people. Did you tell the other person you were sorry? That is all you can do. You can't take away a past wrong. Mentally apologize to that person. Picture them as clearly as you can at the time of the incident you regret. Send a silent, loving apology into the air, directing it toward that person as though he was standing in front of you. Or, offer the

apology to the Supreme Spirit. Accept forgiveness in return. Let the person treat you as kindly and lovingly as you would now like to be toward him.

3. We don't always know if we made a right choice or not. All we can tell is the outcome from the choice that *was* made. Concentrate on sending loving thoughts to the person involved or to the circumstances that you question. You made what seemed to be the best choice at the time.

4. The complexities of communication cause untold distress and misunderstandings. A statement as simple as "I like your dress," can be interpreted in numerous ways: "Oh, how nice; that person likes what I'm wearing. That makes me feel good!" or, "He doesn't really like it; I can tell by his tone of voice. I wish that he hadn't said anything; now I feel unattractive."—"I wonder if he means that or if he's just trying to be nice," or, "That compliment means that he must want me to do something for him. I wonder what it will be?" Or even, "I wish that he didn't look at me like something he wants as a snack." All those reactions are over four words that *should* mean just that the dress is a nice one—nothing else.

If you had a misunderstanding, it isn't much of a surprise. If it was something that happened long ago, then you may not be able to go back to the person and straighten out the situation. And sometimes it is best to leave a miscommunication alone rather than add to the problem. Not everyone will understand the intention behind your words and deeds.

Clear it with yourself first. If you meant something kindly, then you did all that you could. If what you said or did masked your inner feelings and thoughts, then clarify your motivation to yourself. Other people aren't at fault for misunderstanding if you were not clear about what you were doing. An example of saying one thing while meaning another is the emotionally packed phrase, "I hate you!" which may actually mean "I love you but feel deeply hurt, and I wish I felt that you loved me in return." Learn to be clear about your thoughts and feelings, and your communications will improve.

Other people will respond to the energy you put forth. Remember, however, that they have their own convoluted, unclear ways of responding. Usually a misunderstanding involves two people, not just one.

A Ceremony for Purification

Another technique for absolving ourselves of past and present conflicts involves a ceremony that helps us to uplift our hearts and minds by offering our thoughts, feelings, and actions into the purifying energy of grace or the Supreme Spirit. It is an outward symbol of an inner purification.

It entails writing down on a piece of paper what you want to free from your consciousness. Then you will burn the paper and offer your past mistakes or present problems into the universal energy of grace.

You will need paper and pen, a candle or other source of flame, a large metal or sturdy ceramic bowl in which you will place the burning paper, and a trivet, brick, or thick tile to place under the bowl to protect the surface of the table or floor.

Set up a small area where you can concentrate and be undisturbed, either indoors or outside. Set your bowl on a protected surface where there is nothing nearby that can burn. Brick, tile, or stone is safest, but a wooden table protected by a trivet or tile made to place under hot dishes is fine. Place a candle in front of you if you want a more ceremonial setting or else just have matches for burning the paper. Have a piece of paper and pen by your side.

Begin by concentrating clearly on what concerns you. Visualize the person or situation. Then write down the feelings or thoughts that you want to be rid of. Silently ask for forgiveness, the ability to forgive another, or to be freed from the problem you are having. Following are two phrases or prayers that I find helpful.

"Free me from my past mistakes, and teach me to
    act in attunement with the flow of grace."

"Take this sorrow from me. I offer it into the love
    and light of the universal Spirit."

If you follow a particular spiritual path, then you may want to offer your prayer request to the Spirit in that form.

Light the paper in the flame of the candle then drop the burning paper into the bowl. Concentrate on one of the suggested prayers, or make up your own offering as the paper disappears in the light of the flame. As the paper burns, the smoke and vapors rise and dissipate into the ether. See your past or present problems vanish into particles of light and energy and merge into the all-purifying flow of divine grace. Afterward, take a few moments to offer silent words of gratitude for the all-pervading presence of grace.

There are often many pains and regrets that we carry around with us. Rather than digging them all up and having to face each one, we can make a general submission such as, "I offer up my critical thoughts and feelings of others. Fill me with compassionate understanding and kindness for all life." This allows you to be receptive to the changes you want to make within yourself.

We need to learn how to forgive ourselves in order to be able to forgive others.

It brings a great sense of inner freedom when we look with compassion at our common bond of human mistakes and experience the path of grace that leads us to an expanded awareness. We learn to view our mistakes, and those of others, as a natural part of our development.

How Do We Treat Our Friends?

Do we treat those closest to us as friends, or have we allowed time and familiarity to undermine our loving, thoughtful, and considerate behavior? Our family may get short shrift while we honor and support our friends and casual acquaintances with tender concern.

I was returning home one rainy day, riding with my neighbor in his truck, when a new, tarped mattress on the truck rack began to loosen from its moorings. We had to stop in the rain to retie the load. Now, if I had been with my husband, I would have grumped and complained and possibly sat in the truck while he resecured the mattress. But I wasn't with my husband, and I didn't hesitate to help. Even though the man driving the truck was quite capable of handling the situation on his own, I jumped out to help like it didn't bother me a bit. And it was rather fun working together to get the task done as quickly as possible before we were drenched. We kept our sense of humor and showed our best behavior at a time when we could easily have let annoyance come to the fore.

> Treating all others with respectful graciousness enables us to learn to recognize the spirit of true friendship when it occurs.

When I got back in the truck, I was struck by the incongruity. It was a shock to realize that I behaved better toward someone who didn't "know" me. I vowed that from then on I would always try to put forth my best behavior toward my husband and those close to me, not just when I wanted to make a good impression.

And what about the casual acquaintance or stranger? Do we ignore people we don't know as though they didn't exist?

Or maintain a chilly demeanor until we do get to know them?

Why not treat everyone kindly as a friend? I don't mean the exuberant hailing of long-parted friends finally reunited, but genial words, a gesture, or a smile of greeting when interacting with another. Treating all others with respectful graciousness enables us to learn to recognize the spirit of true friendship when it occurs. No one is committed to a lifelong friendship because of a smile, but it may spark the beginning of one.

Be friends with your own self. Be a friend to others. Include your spouse and family members in your friendship. Expand your friendship outward to embrace intimate friends, casual acquaintances, and passersby. Develop friendship as a whole view of life. If we work *with* life, we will stay in harmony with grace.

Respect: An Essential Ingredient of Friendship

To be a friend, you must act like a friend. You can't just tell someone that you are his friend without supporting the friendship with your actions.

Grace in friendships is a pathway for expressing love and respect. We all appreciate friends who are loyal, emotionally supportive, generous of spirit, and who show their appreciation and gratitude. Love can blossom between friends, and respect for one another heightens a mutual appreciation.

Respect is actually the first essential element to any healthy relationship. We usually think of love as having the utmost importance, but love alone is not enough. Love is a feeling that can intensify and wane through life's course of events. But respect unites the heart's feelings with the clarity of thought. With heart and mind united, our feelings of love can be carried along over troubled times. When love is reinforced with respect, a relationship can continue to deepen and build through the passing years.

The Power of Respect

Because respect is one of the strongest links between the heart and the mind, it brings our thoughts and feelings to a central point of greater understanding and calm acceptance of realities other than our own. The person who is anchored in a respectful approach to all life will be able to rely on the strength of that quality even during emotional upheaval and mental turmoil. It is a priceless boon.

What happens when we don't respect others? We let our emotions and harsh thoughts take control of our lives, which has a harmful effect.

Feelings of hatred, anger, jealousy, and resentment toward another will do more damage to yourself than it ever will to the other person. It will take away your own peace of mind, ability to love, feelings of compassion and kindness toward others, and your tender, caring thoughts. It leaves you bereft of happiness.

Reacting to others emotionally or mentally won't help

them change. Furthermore, if we live immersed in feelings and thoughts that blame others for our own plight, we deplete the energy necessary to turn ourselves in a positive direction. Respect is the primary tool that helps us temper our reactions to other people and to life in general.

Is Your Way the "Right" Way?

All people face the same types of challenges in life, but their responses can be at extreme ends of the spectrum. One person may respond to a particular trial or situation with inner determination, resolution, and inspiration, while another person shrinks from the same trial in a complaining, helpless, blaming attitude. You may prefer one reaction to another or dislike a person for his negative behavior, but how many of us have never made a mistake or never acted inconsiderately or ungraciously toward others?

Whatever others do that challenge our respect for them, we have to do our best to let it go. Otherwise, it will continue to plague our lives with unhappiness.

How Can I Respect *That*?

How do you feel respect for someone who has behaved in a manner you can't condone? You don't have to like, or love, a person to respect them. Develop an *impersonal* respect toward others.

Whenever I think about or talk with someone whose actions I believe are atrocious, I try to distance myself from that person—both emotionally and physically.

Impersonal respect looks at the broadest reality with the understanding that, yes, there are people, and also animals and plants, that are very destructive, but there is also the good in life. Goodness can be found, in some small measure, in all forms of creation—even "the worst." We can learn to see that all life has value, even if the value comes from that person or life form showing others how *not* to be.

Try to be impartial in showing respect to other people and other forms of life. It is nearly impossible to give a loving, personal respect to each individual or each form of creation. We have too many of our own ingrained preferences, codes of behavior, and moral standards that we live by to be able to accept all others against our personal standards.

A few times in my life I've suddenly come upon a big rattlesnake in the brush. I don't stand there admiring it, thinking about what a lovely, poisonous reptile it is, and how fascinating is its rattling tail—I want to get away from it as quickly as possible. No rattlesnake has seemed overjoyed by my presence either. They would rather be left alone.

I prefer to respect rattlesnakes from a distance. And some people are about as appealing to me as rattlesnakes, so I just try to respect them from about the same distance. I, personally, wouldn't miss rattlesnakes if they didn't exist in my own life. But relationships in life differ widely. What is intolerable to one person is of no consequence to another.

A friend of mine, in contrast to my way of thinking, isn't bothered by rattlesnakes in the least. She and her husband once had a summer job where they would go out into the Arizona desert at night to catch venomous diamondback rattlesnakes, deadly coral snakes, or any other snake they could find for a study on snake populations and species in various quadrants of the desert. They would catch the snakes, put them in gunnysacks or snake boxes, and set them on the backseat or the floor of their old Volkswagen Bug while they bounced along on dirt roads searching for more specimens.

One evening, the opening of a bag worked loose, and what appeared to be a coral snake slithered out from under the front seat. Now, my dialogue would not run, "Oh, sweetheart, look at this! The snakes are getting out of their bags...and they seem distressed from their confinement." I would more likely emit a few choice words, punctuated by a scream or two, and either be petrified with fright or look like a person in a high-speed film who is being ejected from a vehicle.

My friend, after the initial shock, realized that it was the false coral snake that had gotten loose (the coral snake was still in its box) and calmly recaptured the stray.

I do not understand rattlesnakes, their behavior, or what benefit they have. But I do try to *accept* rattlesnakes and let go of any personal opinion or emotional response (like fear) that will prejudice my feelings.

I apply the same technique to people whose actions are so foreign to my nature that I am not able to understand them. I try to accept that their actions are acceptable to them, and then I keep my personal feelings out of the picture. It requires a form of mental and emotional discipline, but I know that agitated thoughts and feelings will only override the consciousness of respect.

Thought Brings Emotions under Control

Hurt *feelings* can be soothed and healed by drawing on the intellect. Respectful *thoughts* of the other person will calm your emotions and help to bring clarity to the situation. It is very difficult to ease emotional pain or turmoil with more feelings or emotions. But the opposite, magnetic pull of positive thoughts can lift us out of an emotional state.

"Do you know what so-and-so *did* to me?!" is a familiar line when our feelings have been hurt. It is an emotional reaction that we probably all have felt and also one that can endure for years, if we allow it to.

By using our thoughts we can draw on elements of respect that will lift our unsettled feelings into the realm of greater understanding or calm acceptance.

If we want to rid ourselves of our feelings of unhappiness, we need to focus on an attitude of respect. Constructive thoughts promote an impersonal view, which can help relieve forms of emotional upset such as anger, resentment, jealousy, fear, and hatred. Also, an attitude of respect can be used to heal old hurts that remain unresolved within oneself. Reasoning can bring clarity to our feelings.

Use the following ideas to balance your emotions of hurt.

1. Develop a mental attitude that embraces an impersonal or impartial view. The choices other people make may be the right ones for them in the longer rhythm of their lives. It is always much easier to see other's lives, and the choices they "should" make, more clearly than our own—but they have to live with their behaviors, and we have to live with ours. We each have our own lessons to learn and our own challenges to face. Allow them to learn their own way.

2. Try to bring your mind to a level of greater awareness. Was whatever the person did based on a lack of knowledge? Did that person understand not to act that way? Was it from a lack of awareness of the outcome—his naïveté? Did it stem from fear or worry, personal doubt, or insecurity? Was it from some inner need or desire for change? That person is probably doing his best, even if it doesn't measure up to your standards.

3. Did that person's actions have anything to do with your own behavior? If so, is there something you would like to change about yourself?

4. No one is going to be perfect in all ways. For some reason, that surprises people!

5. If someone has made an outrageous mistake or behaved terribly, at least be grateful that *he* made the blunder and not you!

6. We can learn from the mistakes of others even if they don't. We can practice treating others more thoughtfully, more lovingly, and more kindly as a lesson learned from the misbehavior of another.

Feelings Overcome Critical Thoughts

Likewise, our judgmental or critical thoughts toward another person can be counterbalanced by focusing on respectful feelings.

We can't think our way out of negative thoughts; we only come up with more "reasons" to believe the way we do. We have to bring in feelings of compassion, love, kindness, or other qualities of the heart. Respect for another can be used to banish troubled thoughts of disapproval, criticism, judgment, and betrayal and foster a broader level of heartfelt understanding.

One dismayingly potent thought that can creep into the mind is, "That person should be doing more...I am!" We may then find ourselves continuing this line of reasoning with a long list of *how many times* that other person has fallen short of our expectations, of *why* he should be doing more; and then the whole subject can be nicely topped off with a list of all the other things we disapprove of that he does. Of course, going through this list only once isn't sufficient! We go over it again and again to reinforce our views. It becomes a mental record that can be played at any moment for our...delight?

What can we do to stop that mental recording or change its content? We need to remember that an increased awareness also comes from the heart, not just the intellect. Intellectual respect, alone, can be dry or detached without the feelings of the heart to give it substance and meaning. Compassion, love, and kindness balance the mind, helping us to develop *loving* respect.

Try using the following ideas to expand your sympathies.

1. Try to feel compassion, love, or kindness for others. Their misdeeds don't make them happy. Do your best to give them loving energy, even if only from a distance.
2. We all have our own personal inclinations and difficulties in handling different aspects of life. Are we so perfect in all ways that we can justifiably judge another?
3. Rather than be bitter about another person's imperfections, we can compassionately try to remember how hard it is to overcome our own.
4. Try to feel that person as a child of the universe, as we all are. Visualize him surrounded in peace, love, or healing light.
5. If you feel bombarded by negative energy from another, mentally picture yourself surrounded by an impenetrable, invisible shield that bounces back the harmful energy. Imagine your good qualities shining forth through your shield. Focus on sending out positive or harmonious thoughts to others so you don't get caught up in *their* mess.

Adhere to an attitude and feeling of respect, for they are a foundation of all lasting relationships. Respect whatever positive qualities you find in others. If that's difficult for you, work on developing at least the outward displays of respect. In the same way that the external forms of social graces—such as sitting and standing up straight—will help increase energy and therefore promote a more positive stance and attitude, a positive, outward expression of respect will help bring a corresponding inner acceptance. After we act a particular way for a while, our minds start to believe it!

The "Dark Cloud" of Moods

Some days, it's difficult to muster respect for anyone or anything. When a bad mood descends, our positive outlook vanishes in our inner gloom.

I wish that we could avoid moods—both our own and other people's.

Moods always remind me of Pig-Pen in the Peanuts comics. Pig-Pen walks around with a dark cloud of dirt and debris hovering around him with every step he takes. To me, moods feel like that drifting, grimy cloud. I always feel relieved when they are washed away.

Moods are a combination of ungoverned emotions and thoughts. A moody person is usually unkind as well as unreasonable.

Even if a woman isn't naturally prone to moodiness, rampaging hormones can bring it on. Moods can descend suddenly or sneak up gradually, but they surely do exist. And they can be hard to cope with, control, or dissipate.

There is no point in ignoring how much moods influence what we say and do. In a good mood, all is well. In a bad mood—look out world!—everything seems to be going wrong. And moods definitely have an impact on relationships. So, how can they be overcome?

We are in an energy slump when we're moody. No one who walks around vibrant with energy is going to be in a bad mood! When we sulk, complain, resent things, and generally look at the world with a dim view, what is needed is some positive energy and positive action.

If I try to ignore a mood and pretend it isn't there, I find myself mentally building a case to support and justify my negative thoughts and feelings. It is never productive to go that route, trying to *think* one's way out of a mood—it just continues the negative, magnetic downward spiral.

I find it extremely helpful to simply acknowledge (even out loud) that I feel in a negative mood. It seems to dispel most of the energy behind it and allows me to be in touch more quickly with feelings of compassion, understanding, and love that pull me out of the "dark cloud" of the mood. I don't know why it works, but it just seems to take the edge off. Then the mood is manageable, and I can take on a more positive outlook. Identifying it out loud also warns anyone within hearing distance to be patient with me until I'm in a better frame of mind.

I don't only acknowledge that I'm in a mood but also I

command that mood to "Go away!" or "Go someplace else!" I tell it, silently or out loud, that I don't want it. I treat it like a free-floating cloud of consciousness that has settled in the wrong place. It works!

Moods weigh a person down. So, try to lighten up. Is your energy low because you simply need a good night's sleep? Well, don't take it out on others. Your form of positive action may be getting some rest.

You can also use indirect strategies to lift your energy that don't focus on your mood: Give selflessly to someone who could use your friendship or help; watch a good comedy or read a humorous book, and you may find your perspective on life has changed after a few minutes of refreshing laughter; sing or listen to beautiful, inspiring music; absorb yourself visually with some form of art or beauty that you find uplifting; walk or jog to get your energy flowing again. Sometimes a little fresh air is all we need to help us take a fresh look at life.

What about when we have to be around someone else who is in a foul mood? Let that person have his mood. If you become engaged in the negative energy, it is more likely to infect you than lift it from the other person.

Some people are naturally very sensitive to the moods of others. There are also times when any woman is likely to be sensitive to negativity—during pregnancy or her premenstrual cycle or when going through a difficult time in life.

You don't have to pick up or accept another person's negativity. There are several effective ways to protect yourself. When you are with a negative person, imagine an invisible wall or shield between the two of you that protects you from his negative thoughts and feelings. Allow your more positive energy to flow outward from your center to lend strength and protection to your invisible shield. Allow the other person's negativity to bounce back to him rather than attach itself to you. If you still feel someone's negative mood lingering with you after leaving the person's presence, you can physically shrug it off or use your hands to brush the negative feelings away from your body. You may even want to take a shower to physically and mentally wash the negativity down the drain. And finally, use one of the techniques for uplifting your energy as if the mood were your own. Replace the remnants of another's mood with your own experience of positive, uplifting energy.

Choosing Our Friends and Companions

Our general day-to-day behaviors are influenced by external factors along with our own inclinations. And our friends are one of our greatest prompters. We are usually most receptive to their comments, opinions, and actions. Our environment, which includes the people around us, has a tremendous influence on our lives.

What types of friends have we chosen for ourselves? Most of us like to be in a beautiful and inspiring setting, but what about the people in our lives? Are we surrounding ourselves with those who uplift and inspire us?

Any relationship is built on a composite of qualities. One person may add kindness, love, and discrimination while the other may contribute sensitivity, inner resolve, and compassion. The combination of the two people helps each individual develop and expand his higher nature.

Find people to be around that can see and encourage your desire to improve your life. Their companionship will help bring out and strengthen your highest potential. And, in turn, your good features will benefit your friends' lives.

It is difficult to remain positive and enthusiastic about life if someone around you is habitually cynical or caustic in his behavior and attitude. And it is nearly impossible to remain unaffected by those who carelessly dispense streams of verbal abuse. If we surround ourselves with people who are negative toward other people and life, it can gradually, or rapidly, lower our energy until we become negative as well.

Most people have an occasional bout of negativity that can be excused and tolerated. But if it is a friend's habitual way of being, ask yourself if it doesn't consistently weaken or demean you? Does your "friend" constantly pull you down? Do you find yourself, while in the presence of this friend, acting in a manner that is the antithesis of your normal or preferred way of being? Does this person reinforce the hold of undesirable attitudes or habits that you are attempting to transform?

It isn't that a particular person is "bad," just that his behavior and attitude can provoke a negative response in yourself. That person may not affect others in the same way; it may be the combination of your two personalities that draws negativity out of one or the other of you. A person with a negative influence promotes your moods of anger, resentment, a sense of failure, or other similar unwanted reactions. These are people who discourage rather than encourage.

A negative energy can actually weaken our will to change our lives for the better. If this describes one, or some, of your friends, are you willing to sacrifice your own happiness to those who regard it so lightly?

It may be important for your well-being to distance yourself somewhat from those friends who do more damage than good. Seek out friends who appreciate your positive qualities and who encourage your higher self.

Every time we manage to remove negativity from our thoughts or actions, we achieve a small victory for ourselves. Eventually, as the victories mount, we discover an inner transformation that emanates outward to the people around us.

Marriage, or an Intimate Partner, in Our New Age

The smiling couple, glowingly happy in each other's arms, is the perfect illustration of the classic fairy-tale line "...and they lived happily ever after."

It's what every woman seems to want—blissful harmony uninterrupted by the daily realities of life. *Reality* is the glitch behind the scene. Where are the dirty dishes? The piles of laundry? The financial problems? Disagreements? And the demands or needs of others that are so often placed in the woman's hands? Not in that picture of blissful harmony. In that picture, even the weather is perfect!

Is the reality truly so horrifying that it must be left out of the scene? Only if we let it become that way. A deeply loving relationship based on mutual respect, consideration for one another, cooperation, and the desire to give strength and encouragement to each other creates a more lasting and fulfilling life together than any picture that captures only our unrealized hopes and dreams.

Can Relationships Bring Joy and Love?

If we can't be happy within ourselves, how can we expect other people to make us happy? Do we expect our partners in life to be able to change our realities to such an extent that we suddenly find our lives filled with joy and happiness even if we didn't have it before?

Just as no one can give us a joyful nature, no one can create happiness in a relationship for us. We have to do our own part. Taking responsibility for ourselves, and our own actions, is the best place to start.

Decide What's Important

What's truly important in our relationships and what can we live without? It's different for each of us. Sometimes, it's easier to know what we *don't* want than what we care about most.

Tenderness and affection from a partner can be vitally important to some. Intelligence, a quick wit, and a strong drive to succeed may be important to someone else. And what we value when we are young can change as we mature. Seeing our partner act with integrity and sensitivity and sharing the same ideals has a lot of merit when we are older, but we may not know how to look for, or recognize, these qualities when we are younger.

Be realistic in your expectations. No one person can fulfill your every hope and desire. That is merely wishful thinking and is not the role of relationships. The purpose of life is to learn, not to be gratified.

If we expect to be completely fulfilled by another person, we are doomed to disappointment. But we can learn how to develop partnerships that bring out the best in one another, which is eminently more rewarding than having someone try to satisfy our every desire.

What do we see in our partners—the things they do or the things they don't do?

If you rate your partner only according to the work he does or the chores managed around the house, then you can expect your relationship to have a focus more on outward performance.

However, if you prefer to look at the deeper nature of your partner, his inherent qualities and how they enrich your life, then you have a relationship based on inner meaning and personal growth.

If you want a deep, personal connection and your main

complaint is that your partner doesn't do the laundry or help clean the house—but he is loving, sensitive, and emotionally supportive and brings out your better qualities—then take a good, long look at what you do have and quit complaining. Keep your perspective clear concerning what is of utmost importance to you.

A Mother's Advice

I clearly remember the day my mother gave me guidelines on how to be a good wife. I was only about 16 at the time and didn't fully understand the meaning behind some of her advice, but I knew that what she was saying came from the wisdom of her life's experience. It was one of those moments when I *knew* that I should listen to her.

Completely out of context, my mother began by saying, "Nancy, when your husband comes home at the end of the day, meet him at the door with a kiss." I thought, "What is she talking about?!" Then she went on, "And don't greet him with your hair in curlers and wearing a skin-toning face mask." (My then-current condition, which prompted her advice.)

She paused for a moment, then continued, "It isn't good to stay dressed in your bathrobe or lounging clothes because you are too lazy to change. Look nice when you greet your husband. And don't start complaining about the children the moment he walks through the door. He will be tired and won't want to be bombarded with a list of your problems and all the things the children did that day. Ask him about how *his* day went. Show interest in *his* life. You want your husband to look forward to returning home at the end of the day."

That was all she told me. She may have intended to tell me more when I was a little older, but I'm glad that she told me these things when she did, as she suddenly passed away a few years later.

It's a shame more women aren't given this sage advice. This may be a bit blunt, but why would a man want to come home to a sloppy and complaining wife rather than a loving woman?

At first, I didn't understand the importance of greeting one's partner at the door with a kiss, but in time, I realized that it is *very* important to greet an intimate partner with affection if tenderness is to remain alive in the relationship.

It is not always easy to stop whatever activity is occupying our attention to lovingly greet our partner at the door. But if this habit is not developed, a wedge of distance and remoteness can slowly build over time without our noticing the widening separateness. It is much easier to cultivate a pattern of warm greetings than to try to bring back a spontaneous warmth once it's gone. Take a look at how you are greeting the person you love. Would *you* feel happy to be home—and does he?

It is also crucial to show interest in the lives of our partners. My mother, after greeting my father at the front door with a welcoming kiss, made it a habit to ask him about his day's work. They relaxed and talked together nearly every evening about both their interests—and her daily attentions to my father helped nourish the relationship throughout their lives. Near the end of my father's life, years after my mother had passed away, my father quietly confided that he had never stopped missing my mother's loving and supportive presence.

It may be more difficult to give as much attention to a relationship nowadays when both partners may be engaged in full-time jobs, but it remains vital for a lasting romance. If a woman is working, going to school, or learning a new skill and has spent a long day utilizing her mental abilities, it may be hard for her to shift into a home role and move into a more compassionate and nurturing mode. Yet the softer, sensitive side is needed to some degree for a woman's personal harmony as well as for the balance and harmony in a relationship.

And what about my mother's pointed comment about curlers, face mask, and presentable attire? I hadn't given my appearance a moment's thought, which was the crux of her observation.

Why not try to look nice for the partners we love? Should they be subjected to seeing us only at our worst? Our partners don't see anyone else like that—they see others when they are dressed for work or for being out in the public eye.

We develop personal dignity and respect when we maintain a certain level of bodily care and attention. Be thoughtful about the way you look each day so the unspoken message you give out is the one you want your partner to receive. Relaxed attire does not have to be slovenly, just comfortable. And being "dressed nicely" can be any clothing that is complementary to you.

My mother didn't quite come out and say it, for she would have refrained from hinting at such a thing, but don't give your partner lots of "reasons" to look elsewhere for companionship. Foster love, affection, respect, and happiness together.

Some of the gestures we build into our relationships may seem at first glance to be somewhat superficial. But even a small action that elevates our consciousness—be it caring about how we present ourselves or how we interact intimately with another—will also add to our deepening experience of grace.

~

Sharing Life Together

There should be some kind of mother-to-son talk that prepares young men for future relationships with women—a new kind of facts-of-life lecture. A number of puzzling feminine attributes could be clarified—explaining a woman's need to be comforted, the feminine desire to share food, the importance of showing appreciation for the chores and work a woman does, and the benefits of relating with graciousness and diplomacy.

Lesson number one should explain that a woman needs loving, supportive attention just like anyone else. Men don't always understand that a grown woman needs to be nurtured. It is expected that she will know to give emotional support, warmth, and affection to others—but a woman can use some, too!

It seems that some men think if a woman wants to be held or embraced, she *obviously* wants more intimacy than that. Wrong! She may simply want to be surrounded by the comfort and secure feeling of another person who cares for her. There are also times when a woman becomes emotionally depleted and wants to snuggle or be embraced to help her rebuild her emotional reserves. When that is the case, a man will be most appreciated if he gives the woman only what she wants rather than asking, or expecting, one more thing of her.

Would You Like to Share?

A man is often dismayed at and unprepared for the fact that a woman may want to eat off his plate. It throws him off balance. Why, he may ask, doesn't she just get her own plate or bowl of the same thing? But it isn't a logical desire on the woman's part—nor are a woman's occasional retorts, "Well, I don't really want any...just a bite," or, "It just seems to taste better off your plate."

Men probably object because it affects their speculative calculations on how much of the ice cream, cake, or savory dish they will get to eat. But men may as well reconcile themselves to sharing some portion of a special dish with a woman who feels that sharing food with a man is a nurturing and cozy exchange. It is for her, and one that she may not wish to relinquish. "Would you like to share some?" is a good phrase for men to learn. It takes a woman's view into account.

Appreciation for One Another

Many women end up feeling scant appreciation from their partners for all the things they do. How can we encourage recognition and emotional support?

If we want to be appreciated, we also need to express it toward others. If we are considerate of our partners and give in ways that are meaningful to them, it keeps the avenue open for them to perform similar kindness for us in return.

When I was first married, I would do some special cleaning or fix-it project around the house and then wait for my husband to notice. It didn't always work. And I didn't have the patience to wait until it did.

I quickly learned that if I want recognition or appreciation for something, it will come a lot faster if I tell my husband, Kerry, what I have done. Then he can give his lovely demonstration of sincere appreciation and doesn't have to pass the test of noticing every little thing I do. And he does the same thing for me. We try to keep it on a light level like, "Guess what I did today? I finally cleaned all the windows." Then we take a moment together to appreciate the view.

It makes life much more pleasant to notice the many small ways we both contribute to the relationship. It isn't a forced communication, but an easy recognition of the part each of us plays.

I also decided early on in our marriage that I didn't want to be a nagging wife. There were some things I wanted Kerry to do but couldn't figure out how to get him to do them. Then, I suddenly realized that if I wanted something done so badly, I could jolly well do it myself! If I want the lawn mowed and Kerry doesn't seem to care that the grass is a bit long, I can either mow it myself, hire someone to do it, or quit fussing about it. Turning into a nag is not one of my goals in life. It is not only an unpleasant habit but also it creates resentment, not support. Yes, some people can probably get their partners to do their biddings, but at what sacrifice? "I have to do this or my wife will be ghastly to be around" is not a terrific incentive.

It *is* fair to ask your partner if he will do such-and-such a thing, but asking and then *demanding* compliance is as denigrating to a man as when a woman is expected to obey her husband's commands. If we're not willing to do it, why expect it of someone else? We need to learn how to work together.

Some people would rather wash dishes than cook; others would rather clean the house than prepare meals. And no matter how many years you are together, there will be some things that your partner just won't be inclined to do.

Each person will have his natural strengths and tendencies that add to the relationship. Find the things you each are more willing to do or enjoy doing.

Some men love a clean house and are willing to clean it themselves. Other men leave a mess from one end of the house to the other and are surprised anyone notices. We can become tolerant of one another's foibles or impatient and critical that the other person doesn't behave the way we want. Our attitudes won't change the fact that each person has his own way of doing things. It will only change how we feel about it.

You may still be tempted to bug your partner until something gets done, but try to find a lighthearted or less biting way to prod him into action. Friends helped me discover the great effectiveness of a lighthearted nudge.

Two friends of mine were comparing stories about the men in their lives. One woman was commenting on the fact that she didn't know how it was possible, but her husband could walk up the stairs past a pile of folded laundry for over three days (she left it to see how long it would take him to notice) and never think to carry the clean clothes upstairs. She marveled that he seemed to think that it was completely up to her to take the laundry upstairs and put the clothes away. Why couldn't *he*? (She finally gave in and did it herself.)

The other woman experienced the same startling phenomenon with her husband, and the two friends were cheered when they realized that they shared a common plight. They laughed about what an amazing and convenient trait this would be—how fabulous to not notice things like laundry, dirty dishes, and other household chores!

I related this story to my husband, amused as I was about how real the situation is for many women, myself included. I had seen Kerry stroll past folded laundry without a pause and could laugh with my friends at the familiar oversight.

Well, Kerry looked surprised by my laughter about the way he and his friends didn't even see these things. I thought that it was funny and related the incident without a reproachful twist such as, "You men!"

And from that day on, Kerry has taken the folded clothes upstairs, helped more with the laundry, and done things around the house that went unnoticed before. I never asked Kerry to start making these changes, but when I was able to laugh about it in a nonaccusing and nondemanding way, he changed instantly of his own accord! He was receptive to change when it wasn't thrust upon him.

Why get upset because your partner sees and does things differently? If our "list" of expectations becomes too long, we forget to look at the other list of all the things our partner *does* do in the relationship.

Love a man for who he is, not who you think that he ought to become or how much better he would be if only he followed your guidelines. I would rather look at the kind and loving nature of my husband than judge him according to how frequently he mows the lawn or does other chores around the house. Those things don't matter so much to me in the broader view of our life together.

The consequences are too grave if we take one another for granted. Express your gratitude and appreciation and maintain your awareness of the kind and helpful things contributed by your partner. Even though the same chores, kindness, or gifts may be repeated for many years, the actions still deserve sincere thanks.

Imperfections: Real or Imagined

One day, a friend was joking about the oddities of relationships and how something as insignificant as whether a toothpaste tube is squeezed or neatly rolled up from the end can turn into a seemingly important issue. It seems absurd that a toothpaste tube can affect anyone's equanimity, but it can happen all too easily.

It is helpful to learn to *enjoy* the curious differences between people. It will do much to bring harmony to your relationships.

Kerry used to find it somewhat irritating that I seem to have a particular talent for spilling things. I have created some truly enormous messes with the slightest move. Kerry would always be the first one there, cleaning up after the latest disaster. He could not understand how I managed to continually spill, drop, or tip over such a wide variety of items.

Then, one day we were visiting two very close friends who offered to make us tea. As we stood talking in the kitchen, the mother and daughter team went to work on this simple task. While I stood next to her, the daughter began by spilling from the kettle as she poured water into the cups, proceeded to drip tea from the bags all over the counter, then knocked into one of the cups, sloshing even more tea onto the counter—all as though this was a natural, though frustrating, part of the ritual. In her efforts to stop the mess, she spilled even more. As she burned her fingertips while trying to cope with the hot tea bags, her mother followed in her wake with cloth in hand, trying against all odds to keep up with her daughter. The devastation continued to grow, much to the shocked exasperation of both women. Kerry suddenly burst into infectious laughter as he witnessed this exaggerated episode of one of our routines at home. One spilled freely; the other followed and tried to stem the tide. We all laughed together as this parody continued to unfold. I had to marvel...I couldn't begin to compare with this fellow creator of chaos. I'll love her always for that day.

Now when I spill something, Kerry just smiles. It has become a charming quality that he sees in me, not an aggravation. And because it doesn't bother him anymore, there is no more tension around it, and I don't seem to spill as much as I used to. And when Kerry or I spill something, we laugh and rate its effectiveness: Did it actually manage to not just spill on the counter but also into a drawer, down the front of the cupboards, and dribble between the stove and the countertop? *That*, then, is a good one!

Having tea at a friend's home completely changed our perspective—both Kerry's *and* mine. I no longer get upset with myself if I spill something, and Kerry just sees it as part of life in the kitchen. A person's outlook is really what counts most.

Diplomacy and Intimacy

Diplomacy isn't just a form of communication between foreign nations. It is the basis of respectful communication between people. How something is stated, the words chosen, the tone of voice, and the timing of when something is presented is definitely an art. In any relationship there will be countless opportunities to refine communication.

Diplomacy is of prime importance in an intimate relationship. Partners must have a willingness to cooperate and give to one another for there to develop a strong foundation for growth and happiness. If diplomacy is not developed or it breaks down, it results in the two partners holding resolutely to their list of demands, each unwilling to cede his or her point of view. All that can be done at this juncture is to back off and give the situation some time to settle before addressing it again. Without cooperation and diplomacy, a relationship becomes more like two warring nations than two allies working together.

If you want something to change in the relationship, ask for it at a good moment and in a considerate way. Allow your partner time to make the change, and remind him gently only if you need to. Learn when to ask for more support and when to wait for a time when your partner will be more receptive. The time to ask for change is when you can ask calmly and kindly. Choose a moment when you are both rested and relaxed.

Take some responsibility for the request for change. Be a diplomat. Let your partner feel your willingness to participate in the new way of doing things, and make the change as enjoyable for the two of you as possible. Your partner shouldn't feel like you are accusing him of being negligent—a one-way statement of him needing to do more, period. Successful communication requires more tact than that. Say that you have been thinking or feeling a particular way, and ask if he minds helping to shift the energy in this new direction. Then follow your request by mentioning what you are able to do to help with the new routine. And keep your word. If you say that you'll help, then do so sincerely. The next time you make a suggestion, your partner is likely to be more open and cooperative rather than resistant to your idea.

Confronting a Person's Faults

It can be a generous gesture to look the other way when a person has a particular fault or bad habit that you know is difficult to overcome. But sometimes a person has a shortcoming that is hurtful to others, so then it may be of value to gently mention it to him. But for the most part, none of us wants to be directly told that what we are doing is wrong. It makes us defensive, even if it *is* true.

Judging when to say something, and when it is best to hold back your comment, requires a tremendous amount of sensitive discrimination. If there is *any* doubt about another person's openness to seeing and understanding a new way of behaving—then wait before you speak, or the other person may just react defensively and not be able to accept your suggestion. Then it may be years before he is willing to reassess his actions.

One way to help a person change in a particular way is by working to improve that quality in yourself. In seeing your increasing development in that area, the other person may realize his error and initiate changes without a word being said. By genuine (and not too obvious) appreciation on your part for any positive step the person makes, you can encourage his change as it happens. A response of "Oh, that's wonderful! How thoughtful of you!" is more effective than hinting that "It's about time you figured it out!"

If you feel a person is not considerate of others, then show extra consideration yourself. If someone is insensitive to-

ward others, you may want to work on becoming more understanding or diplomatic. If a person is displaying grave
faults, your example of a better way to behave may help him
to awaken to a new awareness. And even if the other person
doesn't change a whit, at least your own life is improved!

My mother was a kind and intelligent woman. She was
not a confrontational person by nature, and she had her own
ways of encouraging better behavior in others. When my father's doctors told him that he had to quit smoking following
a serious heart attack, my mother naturally wanted him to
take care of his health. Soon, though, she discovered that my
father was starting to smoke secretively when no one was
around. This prompted my mother to instigate a charming
conspiracy toward my father that lasted for nearly 20 years.

She took my sister and me aside and explained the situation. Her idea was that if we pretended not to know that our
father was smoking, he would be forced to hide the fact. Then
he could only smoke when no one would see him—and therefore not as often. So, until the end of his life, our father had to
sneak cigarettes in the bathroom to "keep his secret" from us.

Occasionally, one of us girls would come home unex-
pectedly and "catch him" smoking in the kitchen. He would
be guiltily trying to hide the smoldering cigarette behind his
back, and we would pretend that we didn't see a thing.

We loved this role reversal, with him hiding something
from us that he knew he shouldn't be doing. And it kept the
number of cigarettes that he could smoke to only a few a day.

This was a mild deceit, but it was much better for him *and* us. My father was a strong-willed man and wasn't one to give way easily to another. He would not have stopped smoking just to appease us. And we would have spent almost 20 years nagging at him and being upset with him for smoking when it wasn't good for his health. This way we all benefited. We respected his difficulty with trying to quit smoking, and it helped us to be more understanding toward him.

We all have things that are difficult for us to change about ourselves. Patience, understanding, and forgiveness for the imperfections of others and ourselves helps us to be more open to changes of any kind.

Are We Laughing with or at Them?

People have all kinds of peculiarities. We come in different sizes and shapes; we have different colors of skin and hair; we have strengths and weaknesses, talents and ineptitudes. As individuals, we are all unique, but overall, we are very much the same. We all experience emotions of love and hope, fear and pain, happiness and disappointment. How different are our lives, really? It is the filter of our life experiences that gives our own lives a different look from the lives of others.

When we set ourselves apart from others by laughing at some quality they have, it separates us from our higher selves as well. It doesn't express our noble aspirations. It shows our lack of tolerance, wisdom, and sensitivity. We chide people for not being perfect in our own estimation, as though we are.

Socially speaking, it is never gracious to laugh at

someone's faults, imperfections, or weaknesses. Even if the laughter is not intended to belittle the person, it still does and can be very painful for that person.

How funny is it to be kidded for the way you look, an inability to do something well, or any presumed inadequacy? Does it make you feel better about yourself? Do you feel better when you ridicule other people for their faults or imperfections, thinking that you don't have them yourself? Not really. Laughter should never be used as a weapon for attacking the frailties of others.

Sometimes, a person can start out laughing at himself, but then the laughter takes a turn toward deeper feelings of insecurity or inadequacy. Other times, the laughter is about something the person doesn't care about in the least, and he can joke about his fault or folly with great enthusiasm. But it is almost impossible to distinguish between the two conditions. We don't know what goes on in the hearts and minds of others. What bothers one person deeply may not affect another person at all. But why risk playing with a person's feelings?

Laughter should be *shared* with others, not directed *at* them. If they aren't genuinely laughing at themselves, keep your laughter to yourself—it can do much more harm than good if ill-timed or ill-considered. Laughter is meant as an instrument of healing. Lucille Ball and Danny Kaye were both wonderful, lovable people as well as delightful comedians. When they made people laugh, they laughed with them or directed the laughter at themselves. Their laughter was contagious because it contained their sheer joy in life. So be like them. If you want to laugh at someone, laugh at yourself to express the joy you feel inside.

Disagreements

We need to maintain a flow of communication between one another. Often disagreements are over nothing but a misunderstanding. We think that the other person means one thing when that person really means something else. You can actually both be saying the same thing and not even recognize it. Try to be clear with your thoughts and feelings when communicating them.

Another difficulty arises when we stop asking questions of and listening to another person. Have you asked about how that person is doing? Is he well or having difficulties in some aspect of daily life? A disagreement can start simply because a person wants affection and doesn't know how to ask for it.

Also, once we stop asking how a person is doing and listening to the response, then that person will probably not bother to ask how we are doing either. When one person decides that the other person doesn't care, it shuts down the flow of communication even further. As the gap widens, it becomes increasingly painful to be kind and caring to a person who seems cold, distant, and self-absorbed.

Mutual respect will help foster continued communication so that disagreements can be healed and kept to a minimum. Plus, respect aids in our understanding that a disagreement or argument is natural. There are times when two people's thoughts, feelings, hopes, and desires for more from life aren't in agreement. It isn't "wrong" that two people disagree. It's normal to want to think for ourselves and not blindly agree out of love with everything a person says. Disagreements can even bring our attention to the fact that there is more to life than what *we* see, think, hear, and do.

When a disagreement does occur, it is helpful to rein in your feelings. Use mental and emotional discipline to govern your reaction. Instead of reacting immediately in a disagreement with the thought, "I can't stand this person, and I want out of the relationship!" give yourself time to calm down and reflect on the matter. Without time to pause, an argument can turn into a wild scramble of defense, a matter of "If he does this, I'll do that back."

I learned the method of counting from 1 to 10 when I was a little girl, but all that did was let me build up extra fuel for the argument within those 10 seconds, and then I would let loose. In those childhood days, quarrels went more along the not-too-sophisticated lines of "You did too!" and "I did not!" It doesn't take much thought to pursue that kind of disagreement. Eventually, children just run out of steam and are friends again. But adults have a more tenacious nature.

Adults need more time, as their disagreements are usually over more serious matters and can have a more grievous and lasting effect. We might consider the idea of counting up to 100, as a friend's wise grandmother once counseled. By then, the heated energy can be somewhat diffused, and we are less likely to say something we may regret later. Some people get so enmeshed in expressing their emotions that they can say things that cause permanent damage to a relationship in just a few seconds of ill-chosen words. So count long and slowly.

Don't let the temptation to lash out at another person win out over your better sense. Control the urge to fight. Leave the room, if you must, before you say something you can't take back. You can state to your partner that you need a little time before you can discuss things any further, that you want to wait and calm down. Then take whatever time you need to dispel some of the upset feelings.

Take full, deep, even breaths to calm the body's keyed-up reactions. Calm your mind so your feelings can be sorted out clearly. Do wait before resuming the argument, but don't think that you can ignore the problem forever. You may want to give a specific time when you are willing to talk it over again. You will feel better if the conflict is resolved, even if the final agreement is only that you both disagree in that situation.

I've heard the maxim that two people should never go to sleep when they are angry with one another. But we also have to be realistic—not every conflict is resolved immediately. Staying up half the night arguing over something isn't likely to heighten one's equability. We rarely become kinder and more considerate with exhaustion. Yet it is also very true that it isn't good for us to go to sleep thinking negative or harmful thoughts.

One way to take both realities into account is to mentally tell yourself to set aside the conflict until the next day when you can give the problem your more calm, focused attention. Tell yourself that after some rest, you will be able to resolve the conflict more equably. Your positive thought of a resolution on its way will also help the conflict to resolve more quickly. So, give an argument some time, and some rest, if it needs it. Sometimes, getting a night's sleep is what you need to bring the whole situation into perspective.

If a relationship is reduced to a state of constant argument over who gets what from the other, there won't be much left of it after awhile. In relationships, there needs to be a give and take, not just a focus on "What's in it for me?" Consider what you are willing to concede, and where you are not so able to compromise. Is the disagreement over petty issues or are true principles at stake?

What Was the Intent?

To heal the breach caused by some disagreements, we may have to look to the intent behind the cause of the incident. My dearest childhood friend, Sue, tried to teach me to play tennis when we were young girls. She had taken a few lessons and wanted to share her knowledge.

My first lesson was on how to serve the ball. Sue gave me a few pointers, stood back behind me so I could practice my swing—and in one giant backward swoop, I smacked her right in the eye with my racket. That didn't go over too well. After a few tears and laments on her part, I persuaded her to continue teaching me. I faced forward again, eye on the ball. She stood back, ready to watch my technique and make suggestions. After a number of swings, I heard a renewed cry of anguish. I had walloped her again in the same eye with my exuberant backward swing. That was the end of my tennis lesson.

Blame was tossed back and forth between us as she nursed her tender eye. "Why weren't you more careful with your racket?" she cried, with tears streaming down her face. "Well, why did you stand so close? I can't see behind me!" I responded defensively, as I gathered our things.

Fortunately, the incident didn't harm the deep bond of our friendship. Her tears soon became intermingled with laughter at the absurdity of the events, and we hugged each other and walked home linked arm-in-arm.

Sue ended up with a giant black eye that she could boast of and a martyred story to go with it that helped appease any lingering resentment. Plus, she knew that I never meant to hurt her and that I felt almost as hurt and upset as she did. I couldn't bear to have anything come between us. She was my best friend after all.

Sometimes, our intentions are one thing and the outcomes quite another. Other than the fact that Sue refused to play tennis in the same court with me from that day on, there was no lasting harm done because she looked at my intention and not my deed.

It is the overall spirit in a relationship that holds it together. There must be a predominantly positive exchange of energy between two people. Otherwise, the emotional drain of recurring disagreements can exhaust or bankrupt the relationship, leaving no hope for recovery. This is also why little gestures of affection have such importance. They not only build up the reservoir of love and rapport, they establish avenues for bringing a disharmony back into the normal, positive flow.

Feeling Unfulfilled

Sometimes, even in the best of relationships, there can emerge a feeling of being unfulfilled. It is usually because familiarity has replaced the small courtesies toward one another.

Fresh enthusiasm keeps the spark of interest alive. Without small, daily expressions of love and appreciation, a relationship can lose the vibrant bond of togetherness. Some relationships become stagnant from a lack of attention and even come to an end through sheer boredom. There may be nothing that is obviously wrong, but that doesn't mean that it's satisfying either.

If you are feeling unfulfilled, don't wait for your partner to do something. Take steps to bring fresh life into your daily routine—make a favorite meal, have fun together, add special touches to your daily life. Give energy to your partner and your relationship. Was there something that the two of you once did for one another that you haven't done in years? This is a perfect time to renew those meaningful gestures. Remember to tell your partner how special he is to you and show it through your attentiveness. It takes your words supported by your actions to create the complete picture of love and happiness.

We Each Have Our Beliefs

We nearly all strive to find and experience happiness through our relationships. Yet each one of us has our own concept of what makes a beautiful friendship, partnership, or marriage.

To create a loving exchange and harmony, give others the

freedom to grow and be themselves. Just as we wish to discover and express our own highest potential, we need to allow other people the same liberty.

In an intimate relationship, share and respect one another's hopes and ideals. Allow the gift of love to flow and build between the two of you and expand your united love outward to touch the lives of other people and all creation.

- We need to build happiness into our relationships, not just expect it to be there.
- When we are willing to take responsibility for our own behaviors, we gain the ability to change what we don't like and to add those qualities that will improve our lives.
- We need to develop self-kindness along with kindness toward other people and all life. Learn to forgive yourself in order to integrate a sentiment of forgiveness toward others.
- Respect is the first essential element to any healthy relationship.
- Be realistic in your expectations in your relationships. No one person can fulfill your every hope and desire.
- Greet your intimate partner with affection if you want the tenderness to remain alive.
- If we want to be appreciated, we need to express it first toward others.

- Love people for who they are, not who you think that they ought to become or how much better they would be if only they followed your guidelines.
- Diplomacy is the foundation of respectful communication between people. Partners must have a willingness to cooperate and give to one another.
- Laughter should be *shared* with others, not directed *at* them. Laughter is meant as an instrument of healing. If you want to laugh at someone, laugh at yourself and express the joy you feel inside.
- If you are feeling unfulfilled, don't wait for your partner to do somehing. Take steps to bring fresh life into your daily routine.
- Remember to tell your friends and partner how special they are to you, and show them by your actions.

~

CHAPTER 6

Our Home Environment

 oes your home feel welcoming the moment you walk in the door? Do you silently say, "Ah...it's nice to be home again!"

A home, by definition, is a place offering security and happiness. Of course, a dwelling can't supply that on its own—it needs its inhabitants to create that atmosphere.

We all need someplace where we can let down our guards and discover who we are inside and how we feel about the events and people in our lives, and where we can meditate on deeper thoughts than "Do I have enough groceries for tonight's dinner?" A home ought to provide a nurturing or inspired environment where you can relax, find comfort and solace, laugh or sing as the mood strikes you, and feel rejuvenated by your surroundings.

What Makes a Home?

A home should reflect what we wish to feel inside. Think about the type of atmosphere you want your home to have. You may want to live in a hub of activity or perhaps a cozy place where you can be with family or friends. You may just prefer a quiet haven where you can cultivate your personal interests.

There are places where people dwell and "homes" where people live. We may reside in a simple apartment, a small cottage in the woods, a fabulous mansion, or a trailer. No matter how big or small, fancy or plain, each remains a shell empty of feeling until someone makes it into a "living" environment—a home.

Each home has its own atmosphere. It may be clean and simple, pleasing and comfortable, peaceful, elegant, cozy, rustic, throbbing with activity, filled with interest, or a center for creativity, or it may have an exotic or eclectic tone.

Give yourself to your home and it will give back in a tangible way to you and all who enter it. When people spend time in a wonderful home, they feel happier and more inspired, gain inner strength and confidence, find friendship, share with one another, and deepen their ability to love. What greater gift can there be?

Sometimes, circumstances don't allow for much control over our environment. Even then, the home can be instilled with harmony and joy.

One sunny morning, I landed my hot-air balloon with two passengers in a large, open meadow in the countryside. When my chase crew drove up to meet us, they were accompanied by a kindly couple who had seen the balloon fly overhead and wanted to get a closer look. After a short visit, the couple invited us into their house for some homemade blackberry cobbler.

When we arrived at their place, we saw an old, disheveled trailer, with various haphazard additions, parked near a quiet stretch of river. But this delightful couple welcomed us into their home as though it were a castle. It was filled with their children and other children who gravitated there from houses nearby, and, in fact, there was barely an empty space to sit down. They were obviously quite poor, but they opened their hearts and home to all of us.

There was delicious fresh blackberry cobbler to eat and a generosity of spirit that I've rarely seen. The couple cheerfully talked to us about all the wonderful people they had met, some who came to live with them after losing their homes in the river during flood season. Ten people lived, somehow, in and around this trailer with its little additions. They were the happiest family that I had ever encountered. They invited us to return again if we were ever in the area.

We couldn't resist a second visit several months later, and we were welcomed anew with the same joyful spirit that seemed to perpetually envelop their lives. I learned then that outward attractiveness in a home can add to a feeling of graciousness but that the real beauty comes from the spirit of the people inhabiting it.

Turn Your Home into a Palace

Today, there is so much emphasis on achievement that many career-oriented people give little thought or energy to their lives at home. Eventually, this is apt to bring about a feeling of not belonging anywhere and adds to daily stress by not providing a place of relaxation and comfort. We need to take care of ourselves on more than a financial and physical basis.

I received a call one day during my ballooning years from a man who worked for a company that had hired me previously to do some advertising for them with my balloon. They were now interested in a full-time pilot, and the head of advertising wanted to come to my place of business, which was my home, to interview me for the job. At the time, I wished that he wouldn't—it wasn't going to make a terrific visual impression.

Sylvia, my friend and crew chief, shared a small three-bedroom house with me, which was situated near a private lake—its best feature. The house was rather dilapidated on the outside and had an old coal-burning stove for heat in the winter; the floors sloped steeply on one end, and the windows fit rather poorly. All the same, it had a certain charm. We loved the location, and the rent was within our means. However, it was a little embarrassing to have some well-to-do businessman come to our ramshackle abode.

He showed up late in the afternoon in a new Mercedes, which did not blend in with the grass- and gravel-strewn driveway, unclipped shrubbery, and my old Land Rover. We feared that he would want a smoother-looking outfit to take on such a big promotional job. But we were wrong about the impression we would make.

Sylvia and I frequently laughed about it later—this man came to check out our qualifications for the job and, after a five-hour interview, left to collect his things and move into the extra bedroom!

This executive had been living in a condominium, with rented furniture that met his limited needs, but he preferred a run-down house filled with heartfelt energy. He wanted to share in our enjoyment of life. We would have gotten the job, too, except the business he worked for went bankrupt a couple months later. Then, our new friend, suddenly unemployed, was even more delighted with his tiny room in our house, with a place for a garden in the back.

An Orderly Home Helps Us Organize Our Thoughts and Feelings

The atmosphere of a home can fluctuate according to its tidiness. Our living quarters are not as uplifting when they are dirty, cluttered, and in disarray, and this can lower our spirits if we're in a vulnerable mood. When you feel like you need to clean up your life, start with your home. It "clears the air" for fresh ideas and new energy.

We all have times when we feel overwhelmed by people

and events and our lives seem out of control. Clean surroundings are a reflection of order and of everything being well-managed. Quiet orderliness may not typify what is happening around us, but a clean environment serves to stabilize our thoughts and emotions. It organizes and calms the scattered energy in the house, which may be illustrated by clutter and grime. We may not be able to control outside events, but we can do something to pull together our physical space. The tangible sense of managing one element brings our confidence and energy to a point where we can go forward with other things.

> Quiet orderliness may not typify what is happening around us, but a clean environment serves to stabilize our thoughts and emotions.

If you don't have enough energy to clean your home, and you can possibly afford to have someone do it for you, treat yourself. Who has the time to do absolutely everything to maintain a place, even if they have the skill? Nor should we feel guilty when we fall short of our own expectations of what we think we can, or should, be doing.

Prioritize your needs. Make a list of the top five to seven items that you want done at home, such as nice meals, laundry, time to relax, and going for a walk with your best friend in the evenings. Then create a separate list of additional tasks that you can choose from when time allows: washing the car, gardening, cleaning the attic, and so on. Prioritizing your routine on paper helps you focus on the essentials and clears your mind of a multitude of details.

Even the most efficient people experience periods when life becomes filled with chaos and confusion. Take a shower to cleanse yourself of any jumbled thoughts or feelings; let the water wash away the disruptive energy. Then allow yourself some extra personal attention like a massage, facial, or quiet time doing something you especially enjoy. Nurture yourself, or go someplace where someone else will pamper you. The visual feedback from your environment and your body should give you the message that you can pull things together. Give yourself some time to collect your thoughts so you know what direction to take to bring structure or balance back into your life.

Yet outward appearances are not enough. What can you do if your home is lovely and orderly, with everything seemingly perfect, but emptiness fills your being? External joys are limited; they must be connected to an inner, heart-warming experience.

∼

A Home Designed to Reflect Our Inner Nature

We already understand how grace guides our behaviors, movements, and thoughts. How does "who we are inside" connect with a home?

We need to ask ourselves whether our personal environment helps to bring us into balance and uplift us or whether it is merely equipped efficiently, like the businessman's condo, but lacking any warmth and feeling. Does your home reflect your highest aspirations?

The colors, shapes, and textures that surround us can influence our inner changes. Materials and textures, lighting, color, and setting all contribute to the energy of a home. There is no single style or combination of colors that is right for everyone, but there are some general guidelines that can be considered when selecting the right kind of environment for your individual growth.

Some people feel refreshed and rejuvenated by living amongst bold, primary colors. Other people seek soft, neutral tones to soothe and comfort the spirit or like a depth of color that lends strength and substance to a room.

Polished wood, lamplight, a hearth and stove, and furniture that has a patina of age and memories add a sense of warmth to a room. Marble, granite, tile, and metal have their special beauty, but they are hard, unyielding surfaces that need to be softened if you want a greater feeling of relaxed comfort.

Do you enjoy an active life filled with a variety of interests? Then let your home reflect that activity if it pleases you. Your home should be an environment that brings you inner satisfaction. Add little touches that will help to bring comfort, humor, playfulness, or any quality that you wish to keep or incorporate into your life.

Dark, dimly lit rooms do not conjure up the same mood

as airy rooms filled with plants and daylight. Our homes should radiate a friendly light that cheers the heart and sets the tone you want to create. What does your inner being cry out for—cavelike silence or a garden of changing colors and light? Maybe you want to incorporate *both* elements. What will nurture *you*? The quiet, contemplative person will desire a different setting from the outgoing sports enthusiast.

Houses with beams bolted at unusual angles; square or odd-shaped windows; sharp edges and abrupt corners; hard, shiny surfaces; metal staircases that are cold and noisy underfoot; and austere kitchens have more of an unemotional, *intellectual* presence. This type of dwelling is often surrounded by landscaping aimed at captivating the mind rather than featuring the soft beauty of flowers. The view might be of city streets, wooded lands, or grand vistas of vast, open fields and sky.

In fact, it would quite likely look ridiculous to have a house composed of lines and angles surrounded by a landscape designed after a cozy English cottage garden, filled with a mingling array of the soft pinks and blues of roses, delphinium, and hydrangea; beds of geraniums, hollyhocks, phlox, foxgloves, and violets; and flower boxes trailing colorful tendrils. The bold, crisp lines wouldn't relate to the quaintness.

A dwelling with arched windows and doorways, domed ceilings, plaster walls, and corners that are slightly rounded offers a more feminine design. Some houses include a curved staircase with beautiful wood railings. The sensation of wood under one's fingertips is entirely different than that of a metal rail. The design may even include walls that sweep around corners, cozy nooks, and windows that reveal lovely grounds and gardens.

If your tastes are more spartan, then that type of environment will feel nurturing and luxurious to you. Frills and lace are charming and delightful to some, while log walls and a stone hearth might compliment the character of a person who has a down-to-earth nature.

Think about what resonates with you, not just what's in fashion. When your home reflects who you are on a deep level, it will have the appearance of being a natural extension of yourself. It won't look overdone. People who visit will think, "This feels just like my friend!"

Add Life to Your Home

Plants in a home add more than a spot of color and function as more than a filler for a corner. They are representative of life that grows and flourishes with the right care, which creates an atmosphere of tender affection. Maybe all you wish to care for is a potted plant or two or a few cacti. But experiment with treating all plants as friends, not just things. This will further your connection with their life in your home. You may even awaken an entirely new interest.

When my husband, Kerry, and I first began building our home, it was in a bleak setting of hard-baked clay earth and small trees. A forest fire had burned down all the large oaks five years earlier, leaving them as multitrunked clusters 10 feet high. I *had* to have greenery around me, so I began planting a few shrubs while the carpenters worked. I found that I kept wanting more of the soothing color and texture of living plants. I planted more and more, until I was designing walkways, flowerbeds, and retaining walls; selecting flowering trees and shrubs, fruit trees, berries, evergreens, perennial and annual flowers; and planning sweeping beds of daffodils and tulips for bursts of spring color—and, suddenly, there I was in the landscaping profession. I hadn't liked gardening a bit when I was younger, but I discovered it to be a wonderful avenue for artistic expression filled with color, texture, beauty, and life.

A vegetable or flower garden, a flower box or pots of annual color, herbs growing in a kitchen window, flowers lining a walkway, or bouquets filling a room with their colors and scents—all will give true life to your home.

Pets or other animals also give us a way to add a loving energy to our surroundings. Children enjoy all kinds of animals. They run and play with dogs; cuddle cats; ride ponies and horses; like gerbils, hamsters, and mice; catch spiders and flies; capture lizards, frogs, and pollywogs; dig up worms; watch ants; and chase after butterflies. One of the first things that they learn to mimic is animal noises. Children instinctively respond to the living things around them. And adults can as well.

It has been shown that a dog or cat can comfort people experiencing loneliness and debilitated health. It is touching to see smiles light up the faces of the elderly when holding and caressing an animal. There are now programs that encourage having dogs and cats as companions in nursing and retirement homes as well as to assist the disabled.

But obviously, the companionship of animals doesn't bring joy just to children and the elderly. All people benefit by having someone or something to love and to embrace with tenderness. A pet offers us the chance to open our hearts to a life, as we would with a person. In fact, some people relate to their pets as surrogate children or human companions. They add another presence in the home. But pets need to have people or a person around, or they can get lonely, too.

It isn't always feasible to have a house pet that requires daily attention and may be the cause of considerable expense. Wild birds are an entertaining alternative. They converge around seeds set out for them and enliven any area. You can use trays of seed or hang a feeder from a tree branch, pole, roof overhang, or deck railing. There are also suet feeders that are great to put out for the birds wintering in your region. And if your area has hummingbirds, you may want to set out a nectar feeder to attract them to your home.

It sometimes takes a little while for birds to find a new location for feeding, but once they know where to go, they will make it a regular stopping place. I place my birdfeeders outside the windows of my kitchen, where I spend the majority of my time, so I can watch the birds come and go. The birds sing and chatter amongst themselves, bring their babies by once they are old enough to feed on their own, and are a daily source of delight.

You may find yourself buying special seed, planting

flowers and berry-producing shrubs to attract different birds, setting up a birdhouse where they can raise their young in a safe place, buying a birdbath or small outdoor fountain so you can watch them play and splash about, and staring out your windows far more often than you care to admit.

~

The Sounds around Us

What do you listen to in your home? Do you relax in silence or put on inspiring or soothing music to lift your spirits? Or rather than consciously establishing the atmosphere you want, do you get dragged down by a cacophony of sounds emanating from television sets, radios, raised voices, and city noises? Have you unintentionally become so inured to those vibrations that you ignore the effect they may be having on you?

Voices, the sounds of daily activities, and music are all made up of soundwaves—waves of energy. This energy can arise in the form of pleasing notes or loud, intrusive noise.

Soundwaves are used in the medical field with ultrasound to "see" through the skin to the inside of a person's body. Ships and boats use sonar to transmit and receive reflected waves of sound to give depth readings off the ocean floor and detect submerged objects. Sounds can travel through walls, floors, and steel, amongst most other things. Sound easily shatters glass and can be concentrated enough to drill holes or weld metal together. It's one of the most powerful forces in the universe. Soundwaves physically travel through any medium that has molecules that can move, including our bodies' networks of nerves, which is one of our main personal communications systems.

Music is sound that we can hear, experience with our emotions, and feel in our bodies. It can soothe, inspire, energize, and stir up fond memories from the past. But it can also stimulate feelings of conflicting emotions, anger and aggression, or despondency.

Understandably, what we listen to can affect us and our consciousness. Music resonates throughout our bodies—we let it in and want to feel and experience the vibrations. "Will you turn that racket off!" is our reaction when music is in conflict with the way we wish to feel.

Is the music you listen to enriching to your body and mind? Or are you being constantly bombarded with a hard, resounding beat; tough or despondent voices; and depressing lyrics? What songs do you find yourself singing or joining in on the refrain? A predominant theme of loneliness and despair has limited benefits, whereas music that rings with inspiration connects us with life and its creator.

If you sing, remember to voice heartfelt songs of joy, love, peace, and happiness to raise your thoughts and feelings to lofty heights. Many people find certain music to have a healing effect. Like laughter, music can change our bodily energies and temperament. Select music that will benefit you. Consciously absorb the energy that you want to experience. Quiet, melodic notes and meditative music can enhance the atmosphere for relaxation and serene activity. During festive times, you will want music that supports a more active, cheerfully outgoing energy.

Match the music to the circumstances. Meditative music played during a lot of activity usually feels annoying, not calming. The reverse is also true. If you are feeling centered, relaxed, and quiet inside, then lively music, even if it is inspiring, can feel as if it were a jarring noise.

We can use music to change the way we feel, but we also need to attune ourselves to its vibrations to fully resonate with its beneficial properties. Listen deeply to the melodic tones, close your eyes, and feel the effect of the notes. Find selections that help you connect with your inner strength and resolve, calmness and peace, and expansiveness. During times of moodiness, low energy, lack of purpose, agitation, fear, or anxiety, put on music that will help turn your energy into a positive flow.

Other Sounds That Soothe

Environmental sounds of birdsongs, waterfalls, lapping waves and murmuring streams, wind blowing through trees, and the blend of nature's voices in a rainforest are a few of the selections recorded for the public's pleasure. Many people use these recordings to enhance relaxation and for attunement with nature.

Indoor fountains are also of growing popularity, especially the small tabletop variety that can be placed nearly anywhere for the sound of running water to soothe and calm the mind. The tinkling and melodic tones of chimes can be heard in any good garden or gift shop. Chimes can be suspended from trees, balconies, under the eaves of rooftops or porches, near windows, or anywhere their enchanting sounds can be heard.

~

Art in Your Environment

Artwork should be looked at with speculation on what the composition, colors, and design do for you. Art can be chosen for its value or for the peace, joy, inspiration, and uplift you receive whenever you view it. Ask yourself if you like the "personality" of the art. If it were a person, would you like to spend time with him to develop a friendship?

Look for art with a message of beauty, joy, peace, contentment, or another expansive quality that you want to emphasize in your life. Some creations depict the artist's turmoil, anger, or resentment or the swirling thoughts of the subconscious mind. Consider the mood of the piece, what the shapes feel like to you, and the energy it will add to your home. Is it beautiful, playful, invigorating, refreshing, tranquil, reflective, or filled with a spiritual light and inspiration? What do you want to be around? "Good" art is like surrounding yourself with good friends—it uplifts your spirit.

~

Interests That Magnetize Your Life at Home

Time at home can be difficult for people who have developed no outside interests other than their jobs. Don't wait until you are forced through retirement, loss of employment, or illness to discover that you had only your work and nothing else.

You need something to look forward to when you arrive home.

Do you enjoy reading, exercise, or artistic endeavors such as painting, drawing, pottery, or sculpture? Maybe you prefer crafts like knitting, embroidery, sewing, woodworking, making jewelry, or mechanical tinkering. Do you love learning about new things—writing, playing a musical instrument, gardening, or cooking? Is there something you have always wanted to do or learn? What are you waiting for?

If you don't feel inspired to do anything for yourself, then bring your talents and interests to the aid of other people— read for the blind or the bedridden or read stories to children; cook for friends, people who are ill, or those who don't have the time or inclination to cook; write letters for someone who isn't able to use his hands; grow flowers, herbs, fruits, or vegetables to share with friends and neighbors. Be creative!

The most wonderful part about being in the privacy of one's home is being able to develop an inner life. Take time each day for yourself to be quiet and inward, even if it's only 10 minutes. If you have children, a roommate, or a companion, let them know that you want this time undisturbed. They will learn to respect it. Be strong but calm about insisting on this time alone. Life's demands will wait. Few things are really all that important in the larger scheme of things, and there is always plenty more to do if you happen to skip something. Our inner peace is vitally more important than the daily hounding chores. Take this time to center yourself and regroup your energies. You will be better able to cope with life's problems and stay in tune with the flow of grace.

Create a spot where you can always sit undisturbed. If you have enough space, arrange a small table with pictures of beautiful sceneries that inspire you or of people or images that illustrate a quality you want to develop. A candle is nice, too, for creating a contemplative atmosphere. Some people like listening to calming music, in which case you may enjoy using headphones if it is noisy in your surroundings. Soft foam earplugs (available at drugstores) also shut out distracting sounds.

Make your spot a special place so you will look forward to going there. You may like a cushion on the floor or a chair that enables you to sit up straight so you can practice the deep-breathing exercises to center yourself. Your time here can be used to focus your attention on filling your body with peace (or another quality) as you take each full breath. Visualize yourself filling each cell of your body with a chosen quality.

Try to go to your private corner at the same time each day. The easiest times are usually first thing in the morning, when you get home at the end of a workday, or in the evening before going to bed.

If you are feeling a bit down, you'll want to get some positive energy flowing: Do some energizing exercises (see page 105), check that your posture is good, add beautiful colors to your surroundings and to your meals, have flowers or plants in your room, listen to uplifting music, brighten your setting with plenty of indoor lighting or cheerful streams of daylight, read or watch a film about the life of an inspiring person (they have all had their troubles to overcome), and give yourself a lovely view or picture to admire.

~

Nourishing Ourselves, Family, and Friends

How can we best nourish ourselves and those who come to our homes?

The kitchen may be your favorite room or only a convenient stopping place to grab a bite to eat. Times have changed dramatically from when families routinely sat down together to eat their meals. Now much of our society has developed other priorities that correspond to a more rapid pace of life.

Although, for me, the creative expression of cooking is over half the pleasure of dining, it's obvious that not everyone has this same notion. Yet we still need nourishment and nurturing energy. Fortunately, for the person who doesn't particularly like to cook, the experience of being nurtured is a feeling of the heart, not the taste buds. It is the loving energy behind the act of preparing a meal for someone that counts the most.

Cooking for Friends and Family

I have a friend who was formerly a college professor but now builds and maintains extensive flower and vegetable gardens and operates heavy equipment. I periodically see him on construction sites when our landscaping projects overlap. He's a dream with a tractor, magnificent on a backhoe, able to solve the trickiest drainage problems, and willing to work the toughest jobs with gentlemanly good grace—but the man can't cook.

I think that he has a reverse talent for preparing food. There is a complete absence of interest and a notorious lack of skill. A cheese sandwich to him is a piece of bread in one hand and a chunk of cheese in the other.

He shares his latest "recipes" to amuse me whenever we meet and once asked if I'd heard about the popcorn he had made. I instantly wondered what he could *possibly* do to ruin it! I must say, it wasn't completely his fault.

He began with a hot-air popcorn popper and a large plastic bowl for catching the popped corn. The machine was turned on—he heard it whirring and the kernels rattling around—so he left to go outside for a moment. When he walked back in through the kitchen door, the first thing he noticed was black smoke. The popper was still humming along, but flames were shooting out the top and igniting the popped corn as it made its fiery flight toward where the bowl had once been. That plastic container was also ablaze and had melted down to a fraction of its original size. The liquid plastic dripped down off the counter and onto a rug where it remained burning in patches. He laughed at the fascinating spectacle, grabbed the hazard in a towel, and let it finish smoldering outside. He's back to eating raw vegetables from his garden with bread and cheese.

No one should feel that they need to cook gourmet meals every day in order to fulfill earthly duties. If you don't have an affinity for preparing food, work toward creating easy meals that make it fun for you. Try to vary the dishes to hold your interest, but keep them simple and tasty. If you enjoy the flavors and colors, you will experience more pleasure with cooking.

A close friend of mine always liked to cook, but her mother didn't, so they decided to swap "chores." My friend did the cooking for her family from the time she was 10, and her mother tidied up my friend's room and did other tasks that the daughter had done initially. It was the perfect arrangement.

If you want to avoid cooking, but don't have a roommate or family member to do it for you, look for top-quality prepared foods. Remember, we need to *nourish* our bodies, not just fill our stomachs. A healthy life requires nutritious *and* delicious meals. It is hard to convince our minds and bodies that something is good for us if it is tasteless or unappetizing. Think about the colors of the food, not only the content. Who wants a constant diet of brown food—can we even feel happy living a drab culinary existence? The addition of vibrant colors, using fresh fruits and vegetables in season, will add visual and nutritional vitality to mealtimes.

Gracious Entertaining

Entertaining can be a joy or a nightmare. It is probably the most intimidating for people who don't enjoy cooking or don't know how to cook but still want to entertain friends. But there are solutions to every problem.

You can invite a friend who loves cooking, hire someone to do all or part of the meal, or order out and then serve it up attractively. For an informal meal, you may like going to the best deli around and selecting a variety of nice cheeses, freshly baked breads, a main dish if you wish, some great olives, and other accompaniments. Add extra-virgin olive oil for the bread—and butter for those who prefer it—a salad with your favorite dressing, and a choice of beverages to go with the meal. Top it off with cake, cookies, or a tart from a bakery, served with ice cream, and you have a feast! And you didn't have to cook. You can even call your favorite restaurant and see if they will make several portions of a dish that you can pick up early and serve to your guests.

One of my dearest friends doesn't enjoy cooking but loves entertaining and creating a beautiful table and atmosphere. When I go to her house, I prepare the meal and she does the rest. It's a delightful setup that enables us to spend time together doing what we both love. The camaraderie of sharing the work adds to the pleasure of every evening.

If you decide to prepare the meal yourself, keep the menu well within your scope of experience. This is true for a dinner for 2 or 20. Think about the things that make you feel comfortable at home and offer your guests more. Let them feel as though they are having a small holiday with you.

When you arrive home, do you like to pour yourself a cup of tea, drink a cooling beverage, or nibble on a snack? Your guests will probably like these things also. Have a variety of drinks for them to choose from, unless you know their preferences. And include garnishes for your drinks if suitable. It doesn't take long to cut a lemon wedge for a glass of sparkling water, iced tea, or fruit juice. The extra touches will make even a simple meal seem lavish. It shows that you care enough to give special attention to your friends.

If the guests coming to your home are not well-known to you, call and ask if they have any special dietary restrictions. They may not eat dairy products, sugar, or meat, but then you can be prepared with an alternative. You may even want to ask if they prefer Italian or Mexican cuisine, if that is what you can prepare or purchase.

Think about what is offered in restaurants: appetizers, something to drink before dinner arrives, water with the meal, dessert with tea or coffee, and afterward a liqueur, if that is in keeping with your lifestyle. Your hors d'oeuvres may be chips and dip and your dessert a dish of ice cream with distinctive store-bought cookies set out on a plate, but the pattern is the same, just less elaborate.

Start your entertaining off right, and end it well. Greet your guests at the door to express your delight at their arrival. A warm welcome will put them immediately at ease. Offer to take their coats and hang them up or show them where they can set their things down. Once your guests have been divested of their outer garments, you can begin offering them something to drink and some appetizers (if you have them). Then, at the end of the evening, walk your guests to the door to say your farewells. Stand in the doorway to see that they get off safely before you shut the door behind them.

When it comes to the setting, first check on the temperature in the rooms. If people will be spending most of their time sitting at the table, then they will not generate as much heat as they would milling around. The more people, the more heat they will add to a room. If you are planning on a full house, start off with the rooms cooler than you would normally want them. If it will be just a few guests, then see that they will feel comfortably warm.

Do you have music playing, or don't you? This is a debatable issue. I have friends who are musicians and in the recording business, and when they come over, they always like to have music on. It's fun for them. Other times, if it is a primarily intellectual or quiet group, I may want a silent background so there is nothing to interfere with conversation. Sometimes I ask my guests if they would like to listen to music or tell them to feel free to put some on if they wish. If anyone seems at all interested, I show him the selection and how everything works. Then the guests can determine the mood they most enjoy.

If you don't know your guests well, then go ahead and choose what is the most natural for you. If you are unaccustomed to a silent room, then by all means play some soft music that will be a pleasing backdrop to conversation.

You can assume that all your guests will want to know where they can "freshen up." Make sure that you have clean hand towels in the bathroom for your guests, a nice bar of soap (not some old remnant), with hand lotion by the sink if you have some, and tissues (even if you rarely use them). And even if the rest of your house isn't absolutely spotless, this room should be.

If your guests smoke and you prefer that they do so outside, then make a special spot for them. Set out a nice ashtray, not an empty tin can. If you don't have an ashtray in your house, then create one using a metal or ceramic dish or bowl or even an empty votive candleholder. Look around your house and you'll be surprised at what you can find that will work. Then have a place where your guests can sit down and relax outdoors, if there's room to keep them sheltered from sun or rain. You may even want to have a small tray of appetizers for the smoking area. The amount of space and the circumstances may limit what you can offer, but do what you can. Your friends will appreciate being treated like honored guests and will be happy in their banishment outside.

The job of the host is to be *with* the guests. This isn't much of a problem if your meal is being catered, but if you are the one cooking, you'll have to be conscientious about this. In an informal situation, that may mean inviting your company to join you in the kitchen rather than leaving them abandoned in the living room. This doesn't work well with a larger or formal gathering, but if it is just one or two people, you can make them feel like a welcome member of your family. If this doesn't seem appropriate in your situation, then have someone attend your party who will stand in for you with the guests while you finish up in the kitchen. Guests shouldn't be forced to keep themselves entertained for more than a few moments while you are on a brief errand.

Be prepared! Have as much ready ahead of time as you can. Start getting your house cleaned up and your shopping done before the day of the party. On the day of the event, have the plates, bowls, cups and saucers or mugs, glasses, and serving utensils all laid out and ready for when you need them. Salt and pepper should be on the table until dessert is served, even if you don't think them necessary. Have a pitcher of water handy for refilling glasses. And have the hot water for tea and coffee ready at the end of the meal, with a choice of decaffeinated or regular beverages. For a bigger gathering, you may like to prepare the coffee just before dinner and keep it hot in thermoses. Have all the accoutrements ready to put on the table, such as cream and milk, sugar and honey, and cream and sugar substitutes.

Despite all these guidelines, the *most* important thing is that your guests are able to enjoy you, their hostess. It's more sincerely gracious to be yourself than attempt to act like someone you're not. Do what you can to make it relaxed and pleasant for everyone—yourself included.

- A home should reflect what we wish to feel inside.
- Give of yourself to your home and it will give back to you and all who enter it.
- Add life to your home with plants and animals, even if it entails simply a potted plant or two and setting out seed for the wild birds.

- Choose art for the peace, joy, inspiration, and uplift you receive whenever you view it, rather than for its monetary value alone.

- Many people find uplifting music to have a healing effect. Like laughter, music can affect our bodily energies and temperaments.

- It's more sincerely gracious to be yourself. Show the best side of your nature rather than attempting to act like someone you're not.

- When your home reflects who you are on a deep level, it will have the appearance of being a natural extension of yourself.

- Joy, peace, laughter, and love contribute more to a home than the finest artwork in the world.

CHAPTER 7

Graciousness
in the Workplace

career-oriented lifestyle can be dynamic and exciting, but the woman who chooses this path must be sure to balance her life. I know this from experience.

Some occupations allow for a gentler manner than others. When I'm cooking, it is easy to make the shift to a home or social life, but when I'm doing construction or landscape work, I need to bring out more inner power and determination just to function in those fields.

After a day of hauling rocks and soil or using circular saws, sanders, staple guns, and nail guns, I don't feel very delicate and feminine. My personality shifts into a stronger, tougher mode to adapt to the job. It's much harder to be sensitive and nurturing at the same time. There is a physical drive needed to get results and reach a set goal.

The day I came home and excitedly announced that I had driven a bulldozer, a longtime desire of mine, I realized my dilemma. I loved driving that dozer! I loved the grinding noise of metal, the power of the machine, the levers and pedals, and the forceful way it moved. But I realized that that spark of desire for driving a bulldozer could lure me into acting like one. The power felt thrillingly gratifying in the moment, but in the long run, it didn't bring out my better nature one little bit! Too much intense, outgoing energy and not enough sensitivity puts me way out of balance. Both assertive *and* receptive qualities are crucial for happiness.

Staying in Touch with Yourself

A close friend of mine teaches full-time in a bustling city. She gives classes on "how to live." People are normally taught how to be skilled at *doing something*, not on how to be a happy human being. Her topics include self-esteem and self-acceptance, dealing with emotions, and learning how to meditate. All of her students are seeking more balance in their lives and want to learn techniques to relax and develop a deeper awareness of themselves.

Two young women from different classes recently approached my friend and asked what they should do: As soon as they would sit and begin to get calm at home, they'd begin sobbing uncontrollably. The lives of these women had, until then, been focused entirely on work in order to get ahead. They had hardly any home life and barely time to visit with good friends outside of their jobs. They had stuffed their feelings for so long in their quests for success that opening that aspect of themselves again caused them to erupt in tears.

Do you hold yourself so tightly in control that you won't allow yourself to have any feelings, but only goals? Do you think that you can withstand this pressure indefinitely without an explosive repercussion?

Who We Are and What We Do

Our society has confused who we are with what we do. *Who* we are relates to our *inner* selves expressed through our personalities. The qualities of the heart and mind can be seen to some extent in the things we do, but we do not *become* our activities. "Who" is a person, not a thing. *What* we do is a reflection of our talents and the things that attract us. It is an action that occurs outside of ourselves. A person's private thoughts and feelings often do not show in his activities.

I was often introduced to people by well-meaning friends as "the balloon lady," back in my ballooning days. On occasion, some people didn't even bother to use my name when they saw me, just, "Here's the balloon lady!" But I wanted to be liked for myself. I felt that there was much more to me than my work and preferred it when people regarded me as a person, not a social curiosity or an item to be viewed with interest.

If we identify ourselves solely with our jobs, we eventually discover that it creates an imbalance because our energies are focused entirely outward. Once we pause long enough to look for meaning in our lives, we may see that emptiness fills our innermost beings; our personal values are all on the outside instead of centered within in the development of our higher natures. We aren't familiar with who we are, only with what we do.

> *Who* we are relates to our *inner* selves expressed through our personalities. The qualities of the heart and mind can be seen to some extent in the things we do, but we do not *become* our activities.

When I was a teenager, I was spending some time getting to know the girls in my new school. They were talking about all the fun and exciting things they did, and when it came to be my turn, all I could say was that I skied. That was it. I tried to think of other things that I did with my time, and it was a little surprising to realize that downhill skiing had been my entire focus. I flashed on the appalling thought of reaching the end of my life and being able to say only, "I...skied." I wanted more than that from life.

A career can be extremely satisfying, but not if we look only at our attainments. The people we meet and befriend and who we become as a person are what enrich our vocations. Working for a business can be a very dispassionate experience. Businesses do not have hearts in and of themselves. They are nonentities. The people in the company are what add lifelike qualities of enthusiasm, a competitive spirit, and a desire to be of service to our society.

In the need to reach goals and prosper, leaders in business will generally look first to what benefits the company, and then, if we're lucky, they consider the lives of the people who help make everything happen. In the United States, we have such a strong drive to achieve that "business comes first" has become an overly touted decree. It lacks balance. People are more important than the things a person acquires. When we lose our integrity, honesty, compassion, kindness, and goodwill toward others, what do we have left of value?

~

Who Are Our Role Models?

The tough, controlling, dominant man who rules the home and workplace with an iron fist is not the best role model for women who want to succeed. It doesn't work well for men and seems even worse when a woman adopts that manner.

Women who can integrate their sense of power or strength with compassion will find a beautiful balance that brings forth feminine enthusiasm, emotional support and encouragement, vigor, insight, creativity, and resourcefulness. We should be dedicated to our work yet still maintain our understanding that *how* others are treated while we are striving to attain our goals is of utmost importance.

The guidelines of grace are all essential in the workplace: consideration toward others, not bullying people into submission to our wishes but rather inspiring their support, showing appreciation, politeness, developing good posture for a more positive attitude and centeredness, and showing respect to all. We must also include the spirit of cooperation and caring for other people and their successes, not just our own. Developing these attributes, combined with honesty and integrity, brings about fulfillment on the deepest level.

Relate to the highest and best in others. You will then help to bring out their better natures. Relate to a person's center, the core of the being that is behind his personality. Remember that what a person does reflects inner tendencies, but there is always more to someone than what is noticeable on the surface.

Learn to see the best in people and to express your appreciation and gratitude. Be thankful for the things a person does for you or any job well-done. By developing gratitude, you will not only develop a more pleasant disposition but also you will attract abundance, for you will be receptive to the good in life that surrounds you.

Treat others with respect. They have feelings, worries, doubts, and the desire to do well just as you have. Respect will bring far-better results in working with people than in trying to control or dominate your fellow employees.

~

Bringing Your Inner Balance into the Workplace

The main technique for staying balanced with your work and inner life is to keep your energy in your center, that point of inner and outer balance. When we are centered, we can quickly shift from mental demands to responding to the personal aspects of a situation and access what direction is best to take. It keeps our emotions under control and our thoughts focused. It allows us to use our greatest potential because we do not have to go from one extreme to the other. There is no need to draw in our scattered forces of energy—our inner resources are there waiting for us. It gives us the instant ability to work with the powerful flow of grace.

~

Keys to Success

What directions will lead us to success? And what are the key ingredients? Work with your talents, build magnetism, direct your energy with your willpower, and keep learning! Do something you enjoy. If you try to succeed at something you dislike, you won't be able to dedicate yourself whole-heartedly and develop sufficient magnetism to excel.

Begin in an area where you have a natural talent and build from there. If you think, "But I don't know *what* I do well," then do something that interests or attracts you. We never know what is ahead for us. If you stay open to opportunities and do everything with full energy, then you will magnetize the right circumstances. If we want to draw success to us, we need to increase the *positive* energy flow. Magnetism is a field of energy that attracts to itself. The greater the flow of energy, the stronger the magnetism.

A negative field is generated with negative thoughts of failure; if your thoughts are focused on how you have not succeeded, it energizes the negativity. Similarly, a positive field is strengthened with concentrated feelings and affirmations of success. Focus on ways to succeed from today onward. Build a high level of energy and align all your thoughts and feelings to support your energy field. Become charged like a giant magnet.

Be clear about what you are trying to achieve. If you are vague, so will be the results. Start moving toward your goal but also pay attention if you get strong signals that you should change course. You may need to take sidesteps along the way.

I thought that I would be a ski instructor my whole life. I couldn't foresee that injuries would prevent me from continuing that career. I surely never anticipated flying balloons, being a firefighter, developing recipes and catering, doing construction and landscape work, or working as a writer. Skiing was all I could envision. What I saw for myself was nowhere near as exciting or rewarding as the reality!

Success requires energy and enthusiasm. If you don't have those two qualities, you had better develop them. Our energies are often blocked because we forget how to say *yes* to life completely. Say to yourself, "I will!" We need our *total willingness* behind us or our energies become diluted or scattered. If you want to do something, you need to do *all of it*, not just the fun parts. If your energy is fragmented, you won't have enough concentrated power to complete tasks and reach your goals. Be a powerhouse of positivity. Say "Yes!" to everything you do.

Once you are vibrant with energy, you need to channel it one-pointedly. Use your willpower to focus on your goals. A strong will aids us in moving energy. It's like the bulldozer—a great force that cuts and smooths a path, moves through obstacles, pivots around what it can't go over, and lets nothing stop it. Let your willpower direct your actions like the driver of a bulldozer. But be sensitive, too, as any skilled driver is. There are more options than "full speed, straight ahead." Attune yourself to what is the right thing to do, not just with what you want.

Always be open to learning new things and be willing to take whatever direction presents itself to you on your path to success. Whatever setback or victory you experience, learn from it all you can and apply your knowledge.

Energy is transferable. If you know how to succeed in one field, you can redirect the flow into a new avenue. You simply need to get your energy going and you will see rapid progress— you already know the steps and determination it will take. That is how some people are able to do so well in more than one arena. They already have energy and know how to direct it using their willpower, and they can sense the feeling of being on the right track to success. Then they go right to the top.

We think that material success will bring happiness, but the one does not necessarily lead to the other. Success and happiness come from an attitude of contentment and acceptance. Our attunement to grace helps us to accept whatever comes as being enough, or the right thing for us at that time. If we allow our happiness to be conditional, based on outward circumstances alone, our happiness will go up and down like a yo-yo, with happiness followed by disappointment and then back up again. It is an endless cycle. The ups and downs sometimes linger a bit on one end or the other, but it's a guaranteed part of life that conditions will change.

Success can be bittersweet if we don't have a fulfilling inner life. "Well, I made it...now what?" is not an unusual response after an ultimate achievement. There needs to be more than the outer experience for the person who reaches the pinnacle of success. Success needs to have purpose and meaning behind it to be inwardly rewarding.

~

When Everything Seems to Be Going Wrong

See defeat or failure as a stepping-stone to success. It isn't always clear why things don't work out the way we expect or want them to. Sometimes a failure in one area leads to success in another. Without being forced into the change, we might not take the necessary steps to future accomplishments.

Failures are clear indicators about what direction you are *not* to take at the present time. Maybe you will succeed at the same thing later, but there may also be another opportunity that is even better just ahead. View your failures as positive steps designed to give you strength, knowledge, and a reason to continue to work on developing your positive flow of energy. If you want to climb a high mountain, get halfway up, and then decide that it's too much trouble to go on, then that's your choice. But if you want to succeed, keep going! Never give up—your success may come at any moment.

When I was around 10 years old, I used to struggle to keep up with the other students in my ski class. I was afraid of going fast, fearful that I couldn't keep up, and knew that I was holding everyone else back. I kept trying my best but remained the worst skier in my division.

The next ski season, the head of the ski school put me back a year. I pleaded with her to allow me to stay up with my friends, but the woman stuck to her (wise) decision. Dejectedly, I joined the new class. To my great surprise, I found that I was one of the best in my group. The confidence I then gained allowed me to improve even more. Instead of holding everyone up, I was the first one down the slopes. It was a major turning point. From then on, I had the courage and will to attempt harder techniques and terrain. I advanced past all my previous classmates who had once left me sprawled in the snow behind them.

Who Does What?

In managing a project, one principle that I strive to always maintain, above getting the job done, is to *never* ask others to do more than I am willing to do myself. I practice this in two ways.

First, I don't give others the worst or hardest part of a project to do on their own. I select aspects for them that I think will keep their energies moving, and I pitch in and help with the most difficult or unpleasant parts. I help chop onions when I'm catering and shovel soil or haul rocks in the garden. When I back up my requests with my own willingness to help, then other people are less likely to complain.

Second, though I may feel driven to accomplish a certain goal, I will not demand that others live by whatever standards I've set for myself. I prefer their willing support or to do the job on my own. If people want to join me, I'm all for it—it's a lot more fun and productive. But whether I have help or not, I take the responsibility or the blame.

I also apply this general philosophy to when I am working for someone else. I do my best, offer as much support to that person as I can, and even if it takes me longer to do the job than was expected, I still see it through to the end. I don't quit because the final responsibility isn't mine. I do a job for others with the same enthusiasm and dedication I've given to my own businesses or projects.

See your work as a service to others, not just as a means of earning money. Every job is worthwhile in some way. Mentally review the aspects of your work that are meaningful to you, especially when your job feels overwhelming. Does your work help others? How does it contribute to overall goals or prepare the way for improvements? Seeing the usefulness of the work you do will help you to understand the value of *every* position in a company.

If you work with others, see your contribution to the job as a part of a whole rather than independent of everything else. Give of yourself to your work, and you will be a much more valuable employee. A good, perceptive employer will recognize your dedication and acknowledge it by offering you new opportunities.

Stand behind Your Decisions

If you hold a position of authority, then try not to show uncertainty when you make a decision. There will be an interim when you need to weigh the various factors, but once you decide, put your energy behind your decision. Other people like to feel that life is secure and stable. It isn't, but people don't like to be reminded of that. We all like to think that we have control over what happens or what someone else does.

Our actions can *affect* the outward circumstances but, no matter how hard we try or wish it to be so, we do not have complete control of events. There is always an element of the universal energy. We don't always understand its workings, but that doesn't seem to change its influence in our lives. You can only do your best and accept that events will unfold in whatever way they will.

The Creative Flow

Creativity is useful in all professions. It may assist in working with people, improving a product or service, in inventing new things, or in finding solutions to problems. Sometimes our creative flow is a tremendous outpouring of energy, but other times it can feel like it is all worn-out. Creative energy in the universe, however, is omnipresent; we just have to tap into its source.

If you feel that you've lost touch with your creativity, rather than try to force its flow in the same way, get it going again in a fresh direction. If I'm writing a lot and my mind gets bogged down, I go outside and work with color and design in the garden or I express creativity by cooking—both are fields in which I can easily engage myself. This gets energy flowing again. My mind becomes recharged more quickly by the fresh creative flow, and I can apply it again in the way that I need it.

It doesn't matter if you do something physical or mental. I use physical energy to balance mental fatigue, but a writer and composer friend of mine shifts to composing music when his mind becomes tired from long hours of writing and editing. A different expression of creativity is all you really need.

Sometimes creativity diminishes or goes away because we are trying too hard. Our mental effort is actually pinching or blocking the flow of thoughts. We need to be receptive to creativity. Take time to relax, and know that the answers or ideas will come. Get some fresh air—go for a walk, wander through a park, or take a leisurely drive. Taking a shower can also help prepare your mind for new ideas; relax and let the water refresh you. Or submerge yourself in water so it flows over your head by taking a dip in a pool, lake, or ocean. It is astonishingly restorative. Also, practice the exercise for experiencing your intuition to draw creativity when you need it.

One last important point: Whenever inspiration comes to you, use it. Even what seems like the most obvious thought—something you couldn't possibly forget—can vanish if you wait.

I'm lucky that my husband, Kerry, has spent a lot of time around creative people. He isn't bothered if I start writing notes in the dark on large pieces of paper I keep on my night-stand or pop out of bed with an idea in the middle of the night and go to my computer to get the whole thing down while the inspiration is strong. Kerry even encourages me to act right away, but it helps that he knows a number of other people who act as I do. The incoming flow of creativity is an experience of grace that should be regarded with deep grati-tude. If we stay in attunement and receptive to the universal source, then creativity can always flow into our lives.

Emotions on the Job

The purpose of a business is to provide a service or an item. If its employees are caught in emotional displays, then the service or production is not at its best or most efficient level. It takes time to express the way we feel, and most people don't want to pay us for it. Communication is one thing, and heated outbursts another.

It can be rough on a construction site. Sometimes I'm the only woman, and there are days when I have a hard time with the impersonal, get-the-job-done-now kind of energy. I can probably say with accuracy that grace and graciousness are not always foremost in the minds of my co-workers.

I've had to learn to respect the masculine way of getting things done. Emotions slow down the job, so men don't want to stop for them. It's that simple. If they are in a mood or are upset, they want to get through it as quickly as possible—and rarely do they appreciate it if a woman unmasks her raw feelings. Also, if a person has emotional outbursts repeatedly, then other people will not enjoy working with him. Even if a person excels at the job, co-workers will add the mental tag "but she's a pain to be around." Emotions affect the whole environment.

Any flare-ups that do occur are best quickly ended. Emotions stir up the feelings of everyone in the vicinity, plus those of others who hear about it later. If someone initiates a disagreement or conflict with you, you may want to tell him that you need to get back to your work but will talk with him about it later. Give the person some time to quiet down. But stay true to your word. Allot a specified time frame for your discussion in order to keep the person more focused on the main points, then listen to what he has to say. He may have some very good ideas or valid criticisms or observations that could be incorporated into the workplace.

If there is something upsetting you that relates to the job, then approach it as you would a disagreement in an intimate relationship. Wait until you can calm down, set up a good time to talk about it, and consider whether the person will be able to hear what you have to say. Be diplomatic with your words. Rehearse the points that you want to make, or even write them down so you don't get sidetracked. Stay centered and positive when you communicate your thoughts or feelings, and listen carefully to the other person's point of view. Don't focus only on what you have to say. Try to look at the whole picture.

The Larger Picture of Life

A dear friend told me about a bridal shower she'd attended recently. She found it to be a distressing commentary on today's "successful" woman. Nearly all the women attending were highly placed in the corporate world. They looked polished, sophisticated, and wealthy. But instead of getting into the spirit of the upcoming wedding and the happiness of the bride-to-be, these women sat around discussing business matters. The shower gifts to their mutual friend were all the personal attention they gave. The women didn't even notice that they weren't relating to the future bride. Their work was all they knew how to talk about.

Achievement is a cold companion. Bring inner balance into your life. Our lives *can* revolve around our careers, but it is imperative to be in touch with the qualities of the heart to have happiness and harmony. Maintain your caring, feminine nature—it's your greatest strength.

Expand your outlook. Develop interests beyond your

work. And build true friendships that are not based on what you do but on who you are. Stay alive to *all* of life. It will give you great comfort and hope by linking your consciousness with the expanded awareness that embraces grace.

- Both assertive *and* receptive qualities are essential for our happiness.
- Our society has confused who we are with what we do. *Who* we are relates to our *inner* selves expressed through our personalities. *What* we do is a reflection of our talents and the things that attract us. It is an action that occurs outside of ourselves.
- A career can be extremely satisfying, but not if we look only at our attainments. The people we meet and befriend and who we become as a person are what enrich our vocations.
- The people in our lives are more important than the things we acquire.
- Women who can integrate their sense of power or strength with compassion will find a beautiful balance that brings forth feminine enthusiasm, emotional support and encouragement, vigor, insight, creativity, and resourcefulness.
- Relate to the highest and best in others.
- Express your appreciation and gratitude—be thankful for the things a person does for you or for any job well-done.

CHAPTER 8

~

Accepting Trials and Difficulties with Grace

A t some point in our lives, we each will experience a major, often unexpected, change. It may be an illness, failure or defeat, divorce, the death of a loved one, the inability to do things that were once easily accomplished, loss of a job or adapting to a new one, or retirement.

Trials become even more difficult when we get hit with a combination of "blows" that disrupts or shatters the normal course of our lives. These times are a true test of character, endurance, and fortitude. Such tests, however, are not designed to defeat us but to stretch us to our limits so we will grow. If we view them in that regard, they will help to give us the energy to go forward.

~

Life's Ups and Downs

Few people welcome change to their comfortable patterns in life, so we end up being forced into it through outward circumstances. It doesn't matter as much what a person said or did to you, what tragic event struck your life or the life of one you love, or the specific kind of failure you experience. The part that does count is how you *respond* to the challenge. If it wasn't your path to take, it wouldn't be there in front of you.

We don't have to like what life brings us, but we need to accept its temporary reality in order to deal with it. There will always be the downs as well as the ups. Sometimes we just have to tough it out until we reach the upswing again. We have a choice between becoming stranded in the down cycle—bemoaning it, hating it, and sinking in the misery—or pulling ourselves up with some positive outlook, no matter how meager. Through our constructive thoughts and actions, the trial, even if we are not victorious, will bring inner growth, understanding, and compassion for others who have faced similar obstacles.

How Are These Shocks in Our Lives Handled with Grace?

All the principles of grace teach us how to increase our energy and use it constructively. That is what we need to do in order to cope with any crisis. Some situations take years to resolve; some will change in months, weeks, or days. But in all circumstances, we need to rely on who we are within to get us through them.

Cling to the positive in life and you will be able to make progress. This yes-saying principle teaches us to say, "Yes, I can go on," even when that takes every ounce of strength and resolve we possess.

Ways to Cope

I have what I call my bag of tricks that I use liberally when assailed by difficulties. It is filled with a variety of methods for bolstering my energy and resolve. Smaller obstacles don't require more than determination, but I pull out everything I can to combat the larger upheavals.

Begin with the premise, "I'm not alone with this problem." Point out to yourself that there have been others who have had to face the same situations—or worse. Never, *ever* let go of that awareness. It doesn't change the condition, but it will help you to look at the difficulty from a broader perspective and have the strength to handle it.

Search out knowledge. To give yourself courage in times of a defeat or failure, find out about others who have had more difficult challenges than your own and yet attained success. Re-evaluate what is most important to you and get energy going in that direction.

Follow a formerly established routine. During larger upheavals, the structure of a routine provides a sense of purpose and a reason to function from morning to evening.

Give energy to others. It will help you to take your mind off your own problems, even if only momentarily. Offer what you can—a smile of friendship bolsters everyone. Keep the energy flowing through you and away from yourself. You can't move forward if your energy remains locked inside.

Find ways to include moments of comfort. Allow yourself to say, "I quit," for a short time until you can regather your forces. If you must wait for a respite, then promise yourself a specific time when you can have the freedom to let down.

Laugh in the face of adversity. Look at it from a new angle that adds humor so you don't slip into despair. Twenty years ago, a forest fire swept through our area and burned down more than 30 houses. One couple I know stood together, reunited after fleeing the flames that wiped out their home. The husband turned to his wife, who was holding their two-week-old son in her arms. Instead of commenting on the hardship, he smiled lovingly and said, "Well, I don't have to worry anymore about fixing those leaks in the roof!" It was enough to make his wife smile back and be grateful that he was there to add his positive outlook to their future.

Take one step at a time. Don't worry about what happens way down the line. Deal with what is right in front of you, right now.

Feel the positive energy. Try to align yourself with the flow of grace. Look for it—it's there. Be aware of its presence even in the smallest details.

Times of Grief

My father was dealt a crushing blow in his late sixties when my mother died suddenly. He had never expected her to go before him. Strong-willed, authoritative and commanding, a keen and flexible intellect, and generous by nature all describe my father perfectly. He was a man who radiated power, and he wielded it with the force of his mind. Yet with all his strengths, he wasn't prepared for handling that loss.

His closest friends told me years later that they never expected him to live through that first year after she died. I had wondered myself if he would make it. This was by far the worst experience of his life. I stayed with him for the first year and a half. My focus was to keep his routine the same, try to manage the house as my mother had done, and be his companion at social events. This lent some stability to his life, but that was all.

I watched my father drag himself to work and stick to the social schedule he had held with my mother. Sometimes he would go up to his room and close the door when he couldn't go on anymore. My sister and I let him be and gave what support we could. And he toughed it out, one day at a time.

Typically, people do not change a great deal once they reach their later years; they become set in their ways. But my father transformed into a very remarkable person in his seventies. Before my mother passed away, he was not very sensitive, kind, emotionally supportive, or understanding toward his daughters—mother provided those qualities for both of them. He could be generous, but it was an intellectual generosity—he gave us money to do things and allowed us to make our own decisions. Our mother would sometimes talk about his wonderful qualities, but he was absorbed in his work and my sister and I hadn't seen his warm-hearted nature in years. It only came out during social times in the presence of his friends and my mother.

Over a period of months and years, the trauma of our mother's passing brought out our father's deeper qualities, seen by my mother when she married him. Warmth and kindness highlighted his generosity, compassion and understanding linked with his intellect, respect toward others balanced his commanding presence, a sweet tenderness toward children and small creatures came to the forefront, and he used his strong will to guide and drive *himself* rather than others. Faced with a personal test, my father used his willpower and energy to change what he could: himself. Out of all of his accomplishments, I believe that this was his greatest, and the one I am the most proud of in him.

I would never wish the grief and pain he went through on anyone. But what it did for him was a blessing. During my father's last days in the hospital, he said to us with candid honesty, "I'll do my best, and the doctors will do theirs. That's all that can be done. Whatever happens is fine—I've lived a good life." And he truly had.

When Problems Multiply

Make the best of your situation, but also do what you can to find solutions for the difficulties you are facing. Stay concentrated on constructive action rather than on all the things that aren't going right.

A friend I'll call Jack, who occasionally works with Kerry and me, was recently going through a particularly dismal period. He was living a rustic lifestyle—the house he was renting had no electric hookup to the area's power company and relied upon a generator for lights and for pumping water from the well to the house. There was an old propane refrigerator and a wood-burning stove for heat.

Things began to go wrong. First, the roof developed some leaks—quite a few leaks. Every time it rained, the water dripped several places in Jack's bedroom and fell at a steady pace above the washing machine, which was lucky because he could just open up the top of the machine to catch the extra water. Then, the refrigerator started acting up. It would shut itself off at random times, but usually when Jack was not at home to stop the freezer from defrosting all over the floor.

Naturally, the generator chose this time to rebel. It would simply decide not to run, thereby leaving Jack in darkness and with no running water. Sound like fun? He didn't like it at all. He would come home after a long day at work to a house with no refrigerator, no lights, and no running water (except through the roof, but that doesn't count), and then he would have to build a fire for some heat using his flashlight to see what he was doing. But that wasn't the end of it—the snows came.

That year, California experienced the biggest winter rains of the last 100 years, which were dumping vast amounts of snow in the mountains. This once-charming cabin in the woods was just above the snow line. Each evening, after doing construction work all day, Jack would have to pull over to the side of a rural road and put snow chains on his tires in the dark.

Finally, just before Christmas, a large storm hit. It snowed day after day with heavy, wet snow that trapped Jack and his four dogs in the cabin with very little food. His truck was stuck in a snowdrift, and no towing company would come out to his unplowed road. On Christmas Day, Jack went out in the cold with his shovel and dug for two hours underneath his truck trying to get it out, but it was to no avail. He retreated back into his house, now becoming weak and feverish from an oncoming flu.

Several hours later, his phone line was broken by a tree limb that fell in the driveway. Our stalwart friend trudged out through the snow to a neighbor's house to call us so we would know why he couldn't be reached, and to try to get someone to pull out his truck. By that time, he was so weakened by the fever that he could barely make the journey back to his home.

That was when he noticed that he had lost his wallet with all his rent money in it. Exhausted, upset, and defeated, Jack had had more than enough of his little cabin in the woods. He crawled into bed and let the fever take him into a deep sleep.

The next day, things improved a bit. He found his wallet after a frantic search, the snow was letting up, and he had fresh hopes of getting his truck out of the gully where it had settled several days earlier. He was still suffering from the flu and hadn't resolved the refrigerator problem, the nonworking generator, or the downed phone line, but Jack felt a little better after a good night's sleep. He also had decided that he absolutely *had* to move out of that house before the next snow storm came.

Well, the decision had been made to move, but then the doubts came. Jack called several nights later in a state of dismay. The problems were getting to him. He wanted to move, but how could he? he asked. He had four dogs! Who would let him have four dogs in their house? He would need money for first and last month's rent and a damage deposit. He couldn't possibly afford to do any of that—the flu and bad weather were going to cause him to miss almost three weeks of work. And where could he move to in the middle of winter on such short notice?

Finally, after hearing his discouraging statements, I told him with real conviction, "There are always solutions! I'm sure that there is a place that will allow your dogs. There's a way it can work out—listen to yourself! All you are saying is why it *can't* happen. Don't negate what you are asking for. Ask for it!"

He commented that I have more faith than he does. Well, I do have faith that putting out positive energy can have astonishing results. I've seen it happen in unimaginable ways.

Jack vowed that he would start putting out lots of positive thoughts and energy to see what he could do. He focused on it intensely that evening and as soon as he woke up the next day.

The results came within one hour! After only a couple phone calls, he learned of a house that sounded perfect for him. He called the owner and within a few days had begun to move into a house with a beautiful view where his four dogs were welcome. And, he *did not* need to pay first and last month's rent *or* a damage deposit to move in. In fact, the owner offered him free rent for the first two weeks. The woman who owned the house said his call was in answer to a prayer, "a gift from Divine Mother." She needed someone who could take care of her home.

Well, I believe in miraculous results, but when it happened almost instantaneously, I must admit that I was impressed. This good turn of events continued to flow for our friend. When he gave notice to move out of the cabin, the owner said, "Great!" He wanted the cabin for himself, and if Jack would move out within two weeks, he could have his last two weeks' rent for free—a welcome financial bonus.

It took all those previous miserable events for Jack to decide to make a change. It took only *one day* after his decision for the new direction to completely unfold. Jack has gained a lot of faith that he can attune himself with the universal energy of grace and that things will happen as they should. And he is now a firm believer that it's our attitude that counts the most. He's seen it work for him many times since then, and now, the first thing he does when he faces a difficult situation is focus on a solution because he knows that there's one already there. He's a new man, with a new life.

~

Illness, Surgery, and Injury

As a rule, people are impatient if they get a flu that lasts three to five days. Few are prepared for prolonged illness or long recovery periods from injuries or surgery. We feel so helpless and frustrated just lying around doing nothing. Instead of being stranded in a state of helplessness, spend your time being productive.

Use the time to do something you have wanted to do but never had the time to pursue. Learn new things. A great deal of information is available on video and audiotapes if you are unable to hold up a book. At times when you can't concentrate well, think about ways to liven up or beautify your room or environment—cards on a wall, a vase of flowers, pictures you enjoy, or small things that bring you comfort. Make your surroundings pleasant and try to appreciate them. If you hate or resent every moment, you will make your own life more miserable, as well as the lives of those around you.

Also, when you are unable to focus your attention on new or educational material, reread books that you have found delightful in the past. You don't have to concentrate as much when you know the characters and outcome. This can provide a welcome diversion from the reality of your present circumstances. Choose books with a pleasing theme to cheer you up.

During a period of illness or when recovering from an injury or surgery, you can actively participate in your healing process rather than lie around and passively wait it out. If you have an illness, visualize healing light flowing into your body through the medulla oblongata (the indentation at the back of your head where your skull and spine meet) to the afflicted area or your whole body with each normal inhalation. With the natural exhalation, think of the unhealthy elements being carried out with your breath. Practice this frequently with as much concentration as you can muster.

If it is an injury you are recovering from, then you may want to inhale healing light and energy into that area, and then with the exhalation, imagine peace spreading throughout your body. Be sure to play only healing and uplifting kinds of music to produce harmony in your environment.

Expressing Our Feelings

This is a large part of handling problems, crises, and periods of grief. There is no magic key that will take away our trials or our difficulties in handling them, but there are ways to help us get through these times more constructively.

How can you gracefully answer questions such as, "How are you?" when your life has fallen apart? It's hard to pretend that all is well, but it's also undesirable to announce to all and sundry the inner pain you are experiencing.

It's perfectly acceptable in social settings to say something that will pass over your situation like, "I'm doing well," or,

"I'm fine." Then quickly follow that with, "How are *you?*" which will draw attention away from you to the happenings in the other person's life. People usually want to hear that all is well even if it isn't. I figure that during a challenging phase in my life, "I'm doing well" can mean "I'm surviving it," or it may be stated as an affirmation for my own benefit. We are all entitled to personal privacy if we wish it.

Inner pain and suffering is a burden, and it needs to be expressed in some way. But how and to whom? What can we do when our emotions are so intense that we would rather our friends not know of them, let alone deal with them ourselves?

The abundance of counselors, social workers, psychologists, and psychiatrists in our society attests to people's needs to verbalize their feelings and confusion in order to make sense of it all. But there are also ways to handle our emotions other than sharing them outwardly.

First, keep busy. We can't process our problems 24 hours a day and need something to do to have our energy move outward from ourselves. Our inner struggles will still be there in the background, but activity diverts our attention momentarily and reinforces the thought that there is more in life than our troubles.

Many people find relief and renewed energy from exercising assiduously—physically working out the inner pain until it becomes more bearable. Immersing oneself in work is another way people fill their time and occupy their minds while going through the process of fully accepting an ordeal and moving forward. It gives us a sense of accomplishment to do something constructive on the physical plane.

Others employ journal writing to express feelings outwardly without hindrance or judgments. This is especially therapeutic when the circumstances require a long time for recovery. Journal writing offers an avenue for acknowledging, "I'm really sad" or, "I'm so afraid." These raw feelings are difficult to verbalize to another person, even when they are foremost in our minds and hearts. Then, too, when we're sunk in the doldrums, we forget to look at the good things that happen—the small victories or kindnesses. We should write these down also to remember them and remind ourselves of the positive events in life.

> Our inner struggles will still be there in the background, but activity diverts our attention momentarily and reinforces the thought that there is more in life than our troubles.

If you can, sing songs that give you hope and courage. You may enjoy joining a choir or group that is compatible with your beliefs and goals. Then you will gain friends *and* be inspired by the music.

Silent communion in the form of prayer or in seeking inner guidance from your higher self can help build acceptance and a sense of peace around the issue at hand. Only after fully accepting the situation can we move through it. The mental conversations of prayer and inner communion allow for a complete openness about your difficulties, weaknesses, and hopes for the future.

Giving and Receiving Help

Individuals and organizations exist who want to help other people. It is *their* way to serve and give energy to the world around them. The people who feel an attunement to serving their friends or humankind in this way benefit by their own actions. It isn't a burden to them; they are uplifted by the experience of allowing their energies to flow through themselves to others. Reach out when you feel overwhelmed. There are those who are willing and wanting to give you support through your troubles.

A very dear friend of mine had been experiencing a long bout of extreme trials in his life—in just about every way imaginable. One evening, he looked at the two friends who had come over to his house in response to his call for support. He asked in a defeated and exhausted tone of voice, "Will you help me with this? I just can't do anymore." It created an opening for these friends, who cared very deeply, to offer their strength until he could gather himself together again. They were all grateful for the experience.

Receiving energy from others is difficult for some people to accept. Yet we need to allow grace to flow into us through some channel, and that is usually by the way of people. Love cannot come to us unless we are open to it, nor can healing, understanding, acceptance, or happiness.

Our personal pride can prevent us from looking for outside assistance. But if we isolate ourselves and wall out other people, we also shut out our ability to receive that which can bring us comfort and relief.

There is a volunteer organization in our area called HELP, which stands for "Healing, Energy, and Love Provided," that anyone is welcome to call for assistance. If someone is injured, recovering from surgery, or has a debilitating illness, HELP will schedule people to bring over dinners for a week or more and will have someone check in each day to see if any other assistance is needed. This service is provided for families as well as single persons. Also, the nearby medical clinic cooperates by having a doctor or nurse make an occasional house call when the patient is physically unable to make the trip to the clinic and does not need emergency-room medical care. Perhaps there is an organization that provides assistance in your area.

Throughout the country, there are nondenominational healing-prayer ministries where a person can ask to have his name and problem placed on a prayer list. This list of names is given to people devoted to offering prayers to aid those who are going through trying times. Prayers are said each day for 30 days, at which time this free service can be renewed. Participating ministers or lay persons will offer their silent words on a person's behalf for as many months as desired.

Everyone needs help at some time. The kindest and most beneficial assistance is that which provides support when it's needed and also offers the recipients the opportunity to learn how to handle things themselves. That is what gets us all through life.

- Life's tests are not designed to defeat us but to stretch us to our limits so we will grow.
- Find some lifeline to cling to. The strongest is one that connects us to our higher selves, the Divine Mother, God, or a Greater Power.
- Remember the phrase, "I am not alone with this problem." Other people have experienced similar trials and made it through.
- Give of yourself in some way to someone or to something you value to keep your energy moving away from yourself.
- Participate in your healing process rather than lying around and passively waiting it out.
- Despite all the ways we can help ourselves through a crisis, sometimes our greatest healing comes by opening up to grace by asking for help and receiving it graciously.

CHAPTER 9

Living Gracefully
through Life's Stages

here is an intrinsic beauty to every age. Outer, physical changes occur as time goes on, but they merely signify our passage through the journey of life. Some people seem old beyond their years, whereas others become more magnetic and attractive even as the body matures.

Grace affects the way we appear to others through the magnetism of our inner beauty. Emerson conveys this message poetically in his words, "What lies before us, and what lies behind us, is but a small matter compared to what lies within us."

The Plight of Outer Beauty

Why worship and value only youth, which is transient, instead of looking at our own, and others', deeper essence? A woman can learn how to rely on her physical beauty to get what she wants. Yet attractiveness is an unstable currency. If a woman allows this social habit to form, she will grow to view herself on a superficial level. Then, when her body begins to show irreversible signs of aging, there will be a crisis. She will think that she is on a downhill slide instead of realizing that she may be approaching the prime years of her life. It's all in her point of view.

My friend Ali McKeon, who has been a professional color and style consultant for nearly 20 years, has noticed that the people who age most gracefully have not based their self-worths on their looks nor seen physical beauty as their greatest attributes. These people relied upon other gifts to define their self-images. Turning 40 or 50 doesn't affect these types of people to the same extent as it does beauty-conscious people, because they aren't faced with losing their primary assets.

When I was a teenager, boys laughed at me for being too skinny. With time, I grew in more ways than were necessary. So then, I received comments such as, "You'd be attractive if you'd lose about 20 pounds." It didn't seem to matter what I looked like, young men felt free to remark on what I should do to look better: "I like you more this way," or, "Why don't you try that?" I attempted to adapt for a while, as most women do, but I finally became fed up trying to fit someone else's image of the way I should appear.

Both women and men encourage society's obsession with a perfect physical appearance. Women may be heard teasing their loved ones about a tummy that has grown or muscles that have sagged with the passing years. Men openly admire women who have trim, youthful bodies or comment on the difference in their wives' figures from years before. What this says to the partner is that they are not as physically attractive anymore, and therefore a less desirable companion. It weakens the partner's self-esteem, which may already be shrinking as a result of these physical changes. Additionally, such critical comments perpetuate the false standard that says that the beauty of youth depicts a person at his peak.

When my husband and I were newly engaged, we were discussing different aspects of ourselves that felt important to each of us. I remember telling him, "If my weight goes up, I don't want you to comment that I'm getting fat. I can't handle being criticized for the way my body looks. I need to be loved for myself."

Our society needs to change its focus to a deeper-than-surface level so we can *all* learn to accept ourselves for who we are. This transformation will start with changes in our own individual assessments of what is beautiful. As long as we continue to think that lines on a face are unattractive, that skin is meant to remain taught and supple at any age, that our bodies are best if they resemble a 20-year-old's, and that looking and getting older are signs of something "bad" happening to us, we will have problems accepting our maturing selves.

The Way Others See Us

We are not our bodies, but our physical forms are the instruments that we use to express ourselves. It is gracious to overlook outward appearances in others because we all would like others to view us for who we are rather than what we look like, but it is difficult for most people to do. People's impressions—received through their senses of sight, smell, and hearing—influence their opinions.

Our "look" and comportment are the first clues that people have to our inner natures. This impression works to our advantage or disadvantage. We can choose to portray ourselves in a manner that gives off the aura of competence and respect or one that exhibits a haphazard, bizarre, or offensive nature.

If we present a disheveled or unclean appearance, people are inclined to believe that our thoughts and actions will correspond to our outward image—that we will show disregard for others, not seek to achieve excellence in our work, and won't take time for other people, since we obviously don't for ourselves. It challenges people to accept us "no matter what."

The initial message we are trying to convey to others, be it through words, actions, or our mere presence, reaches people more effectively when we adhere to a pleasing appearance.

What Is Attractiveness and How Do We Develop It?

First of all, we need to take care of ourselves. We are each given only one body, and it has to last us our entire lifetime.

If we abuse it, neglect it, or ignore it, we don't have the option to trade it in for a new model. And we often don't heed the warning signals that our bodies give us when we abuse them through our behavior. Or perhaps someone may tell us, but that doesn't mean that we'll listen.

When I was 20, I was rapidly developing back problems from physical stress. The doctor who had been monitoring my condition for a few years told me that I had to stop skiing, as my back couldn't take the strain anymore. That didn't match what I wanted to do, and he could see that I was intending to ignore his advice. Finally, he looked at me pointedly and said, "Nancy, if you don't stop, you will be in a wheelchair by the time you are 40!" He was the head of sports medicine at the University of Washington, and I knew that he wasn't joking around. I quit skiing from that very moment.

Unfortunately, most of us tend to ignore the small warnings that tell us that we should be taking better care of ourselves. But as our bodies mature, they become less resilient, and we eventually notice the results of eating an unhealthy diet, a lack of exercise, and other habits that lead to excessive strain on our physical and mental health.

With some women, the less ideal they look, the more they ignore their appearances. The concept of "it doesn't matter how I look" *is* true on a fundamental level—our essence *is* more than our superficial covering—but when we disregard our bodies by thinking that they are not a part of ourselves, we miss the element of self-respect. Our bodies are our personal vehicles that we have been given to transport us through life. How we treat them reflects our self-image.

~

Clothe Your Spirit

The greatest beauty is an inner beauty, and yet few of us have been taught how to define our inner qualities through a process of self-evaluation. Grace allows us to explore and develop the beauty of our spirits so they can shine forth and tell the world who we really are. When we know and appreciate our unique characteristics, we can learn to express this individuality in a natural way, and our outer appearances then become an expression of our inner consciousness.

Beyond Fashion to Authentic Self-Expression

Women want to feel fashionable and stylish at any age. After around our mid-thirties, it looks more appropriate to go beyond current fashion trends to our own personal style statements.

An example is a woman in her seventies who dresses in a smart or snappy fashion in keeping with her personality. Her style may happen to be in fashion, but she will incorporate from current trends only what reflects her true nature. Silver tennis shoes may look terrific on her, but only because they mirror a sparkly, outgoing, and sporty personality.

Make use of the language of clothes. We are seen more clearly when we dress to reflect our inner natures.

Choosing Our Style

How do we know what style is best when there are so many to choose from?

There are basic style categories that represent different types of people. We all fall into one or more of these divisions, yet not everyone ends up looking alike who is in that same classification. There will always be a unique statement for each individual.

Pick one style that seems to represent you from the following list of style types. Then, look to see if you have one or two supplementary styles. For example, you may feel most at ease with sporty-natural for daily attire but like to dress elegantly, too.

- Sporty-Natural
- Classic
- Dramatic
- Sensual

- Elegant
- Feminine
- Creative
- Tailored

Following are some examples of women who have adopted a style statement in harmony with their inner natures.

- Janet Reno: Tailored
- Barbra Walters: Tailored and Elegant
- Diane Sawyer: Elegant and Feminine
- Elizabeth Taylor: Dramatic and Sensual
- Lauren Hutton: Sporty-Natural and Sensual
- Whoopi Goldberg: Dramatic and Creative

By defining our look, we will feel more centered in ourselves, and it will bring out our individuality to a far-greater extent. Audrey Hepburn was feminine and elegant, but she had a different look than does Diane Sawyer, who has those same qualities. And both reflect a unique grace.

Clothing that is out of tune with our natures sends out a confusing message or acts like a mask. If Whoopi Goldberg attired herself in a conservative, tailored suit with shoes and purse that accented it perfectly, people would wonder what character she was playing.

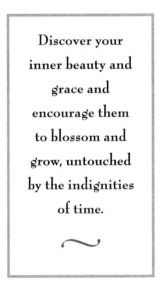

Discover your inner beauty and grace and encourage them to blossom and grow, untouched by the indignities of time.

And if Janet Reno decided to wear a flourish of scarves, flashy earrings, jangling bracelets, and a dramatic, flowing outfit, her inner strength would be hidden behind all the trappings. People would be so distracted by her clothes and accessories that they would hardly hear a word she said. Then try to picture Elizabeth Taylor in jeans, a cotton turtleneck, down vest, and knee-high rubber boots. People would be shocked by the incongruity.

Stay true to yourself and you will have a lifelong style and shopping guide. Fashions change, but style is timeless—it is an extension of ourselves. If you are feminine, ask yourself if whatever you are purchasing makes that statement in some way: Is the color feminine? Does the fabric have a delicate softness or movement? If there is a pattern, is it feminine or is it more sporty or woodsy?

Choose accessories, colors, designs, and patterns that go with your personal style statement. The color pink and floral patterns are primarily feminine and not tailored. Whereas brown and tweeds are essentially tailored.

Jewelry contributes to our image as well. A strand of pearls is feminine, elegant, and classic and will not be viewed as creative or dramatic. Wooden jewelry is sporty and natural rather than elegant or feminine.

Look at the various elements of attire that you assemble in order to make a cohesive statement. Some days, you may resonate more with one of your aspects than another, and your clothes and accessories can shift accordingly.

Expressing Feminine Appeal

In addition to the basic style types, there is also the dimension of feminine appeal. There are times and circumstances when we want to strongly project our feminine side. We can thoughtfully choose to express this in three ways, according to what is most comfortable and appropriate for us. Different fabrics will enhance each style.

Radiant: Many women in our era want to express their femininity in this manner. This style heightens our magnetism in a feminine yet nonsexual way. Our inner radiance shines out.

Look for reflective fabrics and metallic threads, sequins, silks, or gold or silver woven into the design. Glitter or sparkle in the fabric, or in accessories, also contributes to this look.

Sensual: Some women are naturally sensual in their style, which can remain beautiful and dignified if it is in keeping with the personality of the woman. Necklines or backs of clothing tend to be cut lower than for a radiant look, and the garments may have a closer fit.

Select fabrics such as satin, charmeuse, or velvet. Feathers are an accent that goes well with this style.

Sexy: I hesitate to mention this category in a book on grace and seeking our highest potential, but it *is* one expression that women use. I'll assume that the women who want to convey this message and dress in this fashion already know how.

Presenting Ourselves Appropriately for Our Age

The key to appropriate dress is to maintain dignity, self-respect, and grace. As the years go by, we need to rethink and constantly refine our style. Our boundaries will shift as we mature. What is okay at one stage of our lives is not comfortable in another phase. Also, styles we would not have considered at a younger age may look more flattering as we get older. Then there are certain types of clothing that continually work well.

Shorts and skirts: The time may come when we will not want to wear short shorts or short skirts. They may be cute on us when we are in our twenties, yet out of the question in our fifties. Evaluate if they are still becoming to you and appropriate to your lifestyle and environment. A below-the-knee skirt can replace shorts for cool summer attire. It's useless, however, to play tennis with skirt fabric flapping around your knees. Shorts that come to just above the knee may become your favorites for your lifestyle and figure.

Sleeves: In an ideal world, we would not feel embarrassed about some aspect of the way we look, but that is rarely our reality. Upper arms are a sensitive issue for many women. As we grow older, our arms can lose definition or muscle tone, and the skin its elasticity.

To draw attention away from this feature, look for dresses and tops that have short sleeves that cover to a little above the bend of the elbow. Then, people will notice only your outfit and not your discreetly covered upper arms.

Clothing size: The ideal size to wear is the one that fits. It doesn't matter if it's a size 6 or 16. Still, people are embarrassed when they put on weight, as though it negates their good qualities. To counter feelings of inadequacy, they may be tempted to try to fit into clothing that is a bit too small, hoping this means that nothing has changed. But fitting into a certain size doesn't mean that we look our best. If there is any question whether an outfit might be a little snug, go up to the next size. When clothing drapes nicely, it is more flattering than if we are straining at the seams.

Also, darker colors look more slimming than white or light tones. A dark pair of pants gives a more general impression of a person's size, whereas light colors seem to emphasize every detail. If your weight is of concern to you, then wear deeper colors such as dark brown, charcoal gray, navy blue, dark green, plum, eggplant, or black. Avoid horizontal design lines and form-fitting garments. And remember to assess your whole appearance. Look at the fit and drape of your clothing from the back and side views as well as from the front.

Hairstyle: Usually around age 40 long hair hanging down around the face no longer looks as attractive, since it accentuates the vertical lines on our faces, primarily around the mouth. It visually pulls down on our facial expressions and can make us look haggard. The length will look more becoming brushed back or styled up.

Often, when women reach their late thirties and early forties, they want to cut their hair to a shorter length that can be styled away from their faces to bring out their eyes. It gives a livelier look and feeling.

Hair color: Silvery white hair is glorious and may be a person's most striking feature. Yet gray hair comes with age—and that is something not everyone wants to see each time they look in the mirror. There are also variations of gray that are more dull or lifeless. The warmer tones vanish as the hair color changes. In reality, gray hair isn't flattering on everyone. It makes some people's faces look more drawn.

The decision to color hair is very personal. Some people don't care at all that their hair is turning gray, whereas others are distraught by the change. And it may not matter to you, but your partner may have strong feelings concerning your hair.

I was discussing this topic with a close friend who said that her husband of 20 years completely surprised her not long ago. He has never liked makeup at all, or anything that looks too contrived, but when she mentioned that she was beginning to get some gray hairs, he said, without hesitation, "Well, you'll color it, won't you?" My friend was absolutely stunned because she doesn't mind gray hair a bit. But her husband sees it as a physical reminder that he and his wife are getting older, even though they still feel as young as ever.

To one person, the process of graying is a sign of aging, while to another, an entertaining change in life. Partly, the decision to add color, or not, depends on how gray hair makes you feel and think of yourself. Everyone needs a lively interest in life. Will gray hair make you think that you're slowing down and affect your self-image? It doesn't have to. Change the color, or your viewpoint, but don't let the color of your hair bring you down.

If you do decide to keep to your original shade of hair, use your eyebrows as a color guide. Brows generally retain their color even when the rest of your hair is completely gray. Note if your hair had warm, golden highlights originally. These hues can fade from the brows, and if you once had warm-colored hair, then reestablish that with your new shade. Going to a darker color than normal usually does not appear as true-to-life.

~

Highlighting Our Features

Women want natural-looking makeup that enhances, not distracts. My style-consultant friend Ali has tended to over 7,000 clients and says that in all her years in the profession, no woman has ever said to her, "I want a painted look."

How and what to apply is often a great mystery. Makeup is a whole world of its own. New products and colors are offered every year, which only adds to the consumers' confusion. Stop by various cosmetics counters and the "personal" advice can vary as much as the choice of colors.

Fortunately, there *are* general principles that can help to dispel some of the confusion. The purpose of makeup is to highlight and define our features. As we mature, the color of our eyes fades, our eyelashes often become more sparse and shorter, and our faces lose visual definition and can appear a bit washed-out. This is why women who go without makeup during their first 40 years may suddenly become interested in a little lipstick, blush, and mascara. We want a visual boost.

Makeup doesn't necessitate a lot of time or a vast arsenal of products. A simple regime is always the easiest to maintain. We can wear just one or two touches of eye or face makeup or the whole works. Below, I've listed several common makeup items in the order in which they are normally applied.

1. Concealer
2. Foundation
3. Powder
4. Eyebrow pencil
5. Eyeshadow
6. Eyeliner
7. Mascara
8. Lipstick and lip pencil
9. Blush

Defining Our Faces

We've all seen women wearing bright patches of rouge on their cheeks and loud-colored lipsticks. I think that oftentimes an older woman doesn't know how much her makeup stands out—it looks fine to her in the dim lighting of her bathroom or boudoir. Along with other changes, our eyesight can be affected with age, making it harder for us to see exactly what we're doing. A friend of mine jests that as soon as she needed all the jars of cream and lotions for her skin, she couldn't read the labels anymore. A lighted magnifying mirror is helpful when applying makeup. Otherwise, when we walk out into the light of day, the amount of color can look overdone.

Any makeup you use should be of good quality, yet some skins are sensitive to various products. If you have any irritation or reaction to a cream or type of makeup, stop using that brand. Just because they claim to be hypoallergenic does not mean that they are fine for every woman's skin. Respect your sensitivities, and try other brands that are recommended for especially sensitive skin. Even if you find nothing that works, you still have your personal magnetism and radiance, which does more for a woman than any tube of lipstick or dab of eye makeup.

The following guidelines for applying makeup are meant to bring you a better understanding of the general principles.

Concealer: Blemishes and dark circles under the eyes can be muted with concealer. Choose a color a couple of shades lighter than your foundation, but try not to go too light. Concealer that is excessively pale will distract from the eyes as much as, or more than, dark circles.

Use a damp cosmetics sponge or moistened fingers to soften the edges and blend the concealer in with the rest of your skin at the side of the eyes and underneath. Be extremely gentle when applying anything to the eye area. The skin there is thinner and less resilient, which is why lines develop in that region. Put a light covering of foundation over the concealer or a faint dusting of powder to blend the color in with your skin tones.

Foundation: Test the color of foundation by applying it along your jawline. The color should blend with the skin tone on your neck to give a natural impression. Dabbing it on a hand or arm will not show you the accurate hue for your face.

A damp cosmetics sponge is a wonderful applicator, or use your moistened fingers. Dot foundation on your forehead, cheeks, nose, and chin, then spread gently for a smooth overall appearance. Soften any line between your face and neck and around the hairline with a clean sponge or tissue. When you wear foundation, it should be used as a base for the rest of your makeup, following the application of concealer.

Powder: My mother always used powder on her nose and forehead, with a light touch over the rest of her face. She had beautiful but oily skin. Powder can be used to keep down the sheen and provides a lovely soft look for some complexions.

Powder is a translucent covering that gives a matte finish. The color should be a bit lighter than foundation. When worn without foundation, it appears more obvious on certain skin types than others, so be careful when applying it.

Powdering is best done before putting on mascara to re-duce the chance of a powdery haze clinging to the darkened lashes. And a very important note: If you are having your photograph taken, apply powder even if it isn't part of your normal routine.

Eyebrow pencil: Begin by shaping your eyebrows, the frame and accent for your eyes—a person's best feature. Unruly, bushy brows, and those poorly shaped or growing together in the middle, are distracting. We want our eyes to be the first thing that other people notice.

There is a simple guideline for creating a good starting and stopping place for your brows. Hold a pencil straight up and down and press it against the side of your nose, with the tip touching your eyebrow. The pencil tip indicates the point where your brow should begin. Check the other eyebrow holding the pencil alongside the other side of your nose. Then tweeze any stray hairs in between those two places.

To determine where the brow should end, still holding the pencil vertically against the nose, pivot the tip toward the outside of your eye until it forms a line going from your nostril and outer corner of your eye and touches your brow—a V shape from the first position. Where the pencil point lands will indicate a good length for your brow.

Most eyebrows have an inherent arch to them and are wider at the center than at the outer end. The easiest shape to keep is your natural one, but there is no fixed rule. Just remember that they should accent your eyes more than draw attention to themselves. If you have a lot of stray hairs underneath your brows, you may want to make a cleaner, more defined line. If your eyebrows are pale or sparse, you can use an eyebrow pencil to darken them up or fill in where there are hairs missing. Use small strokes to feather in the color as opposed to drawing thick lines.

Alternately, you can have your eyebrows dyed by a qualified hairdresser. If their color is ordinarily a warm brown, then be sure to stay with warmer tones. The same holds true if they are a cooler ash tone—remain with a cool color. Your hair and brow tint ought to relate to one another even if they are not identical.

Eyeshadow: Eyeshadow is used for brightening the eyes. Short of going into an entire chapter on eyeshadow colors and the various ways to apply them for different-shaped eyes, I'll focus on the basic tones that will highlight the eyes when applied on the lid and crease of the eye.

The safest rule is to use neutral colors. If you have hazel, brown, or green eyes, then wear shadows in vanilla-beige or brown tones. If your eyes are blue or blue-green, then apply grays, taupes, and white-beige shadows.

Eyeliner: Use eyeliner when you want to define the shape of your eyes. Some women won't leave their homes without wearing it, whereas others reserve it for special occasions or evening wear. If you are having your photo taken, eyeliner will lend emphasis to your eyes.

Eyeliner color is easy to choose. Match the eyeliner to the color of the dark rim around your iris (the colored part of your eye). This color will complement and define your eyes. An eyeliner color that matches your hair or outfit will appear contrived more than natural.

Where to draw the line on the upper lid depends largely on the shape of your eyes and whether they are close together or far apart. It is very personalized. But *all* women can wear eyeliner on their lower lids. First, draw a thin line starting at the inside of the eye just under where your lashes begin, not at the inside corner. Continue the line to the outside corner of the eye, right up to the point where it joins your upper lid. Place the color *under* your lashes, not on the wet part of the rim of your eyelid. Use a cotton swab to clean up any irregularities or to make the line thinner. Avoid tugging on the fragile skin under the eye when applying or removing eyeliner and other makeup.

Mascara: Mascara lightly thickens and darkens the eyelashes. Select one of three basic colors: black, dark brown, or charcoal. Other colors are fun but won't appear natural and are best worn by women under 40.

Use mascara primarily on the top lashes and apply it after putting on eyeshadow or eyeliner (if you want to use them). If you like using an eyelash curler, be sure to do this *before* applying the mascara to ensure that you do not damage the lashes by bending them when they are rigid.

Some women can wear mascara on their lower lashes, but others will find that it smears. To keep mascara from clumping your lashes together, after application, use a mascara brush or soft-bristled toothbrush (reserved only for this use) to separate the lashes. Tidy up any smudges with a cotton swab.

Lipstick and lip pencil: Lipstick is the fastest way to enliven our faces. One or two lipstick colors is all you may want. The choice of tint is very individual and depends upon components such as skin coloring and hair and eye color. There are two divisions of colors: the warm tones and the cool shades. Warm reds are: coral, clear red, brick red, rust colors, and orange tones. Cool reds are: pink, rose, plum, and berry tones.

Lip pencil is good for adding more shape definition around the lips. The color can match the lipstick, or it can be a shade darker but in the same tone. Depending on the shape of your lips, it may be used to outline only the top or bottom lip, or both. Also, it creates a great base underneath your regular lipstick. Lip pencil will not only add a depth to the color of your lipstick but also helps it to stay on longer.

Blush: Exactly where blush is placed will differ according to your facial structure and features. There is no single rule that will fit every woman's face. A professional cosmetologist can give you specifics if you wish them.

Wear enough blush that you can see the extra hint of color. The amount will vary depending upon the lighting and circumstances. If you are lecturing to a roomful of people, then it takes more color to project your features, whereas if you are relating to people close-up, what looks pleasing in a well-lit mirror will be plenty.

The impression from the amount and tone should resemble your natural coloring, as though you just came in from a run and the color undertone of your skin has been heightened. A great trick to natural-looking makeup is to blend or fuzz the edges so you don't see a stark line where blush or foundation color begins. Soften the edges with a cosmetics sponge or with a few strokes of your fingertips.

The color of your blush should be in the same tones as your lipstick. Use a cool-toned lipstick with a cool-toned blush. If you have chosen a lipstick from the cool-reds list, then select a pink, rose, or plum blush. A brick-red lipstick will blend with a blush in a warm tone. The colors don't need to match, just relate to one another. Warm tones are: coral, peach, and russet. Cool tones are: pink, rose, and plum.

Nail polish: Though it's not on our list and isn't really considered "makeup," nail polish can enhance your overall appearance. Be sure that your nail color choice relates to your lipstick and blush, either as a cooler tone or warmer tint—avoid combining the two. Refer to a color chart for lipsticks, available at department store cosmetic counters, to get a broader idea of nail polish choices. The polish color doesn't need to be identical to your lipstick but can be if you prefer.

In the evening: And finally, refresh your makeup if you are going out in the evening. The lighting is dimmer after dark, so you will want to apply a little more of everything.

Lipstick may be used more generously, blotting it only lightly with a tissue. Or enhance the color with a lip pencil in a slightly darker shade either under the lipstick or outlining your lips.

Wear a metallic highlighter under the arch of your brows

for more luminous eyes. Use an iridescent version of your white-beige or vanilla-beige eyeshadow.

You may not wear blush in the daytime, but in the evening, it will add a nice touch of color. Then, for a more finished, dressy look, apply powder to your face.

At the end of the day, make it a habit to remove makeup before you go to sleep. Skin needs fresh air, gentle cleansing, and moisturizing to remain healthy. Lashes, too, can become brittle if mascara is left on all the time. Eye-makeup remover is nice to use, as it is formulated for the delicate area around the eyes. A moisturizing eye cream is also good to put on afterward in order to replenish this sensitive skin during the hours of rest.

An Expression of Harmony and Contentment

Clothes and makeup are a large part of a woman's visual image, but not all. Softness is added with the heart's qualities, not by adorning lace and lipstick. Self-acceptance lends a look of strength and courage more so than do strident words and a hardened manner. Contentment adds a harmonious glow to our being. And laughter protects us from the hard lines of bitterness.

Our View of Life

Change your view of life's course. There is no "going downhill." All of life is a progressive journey. Our life spans are getting longer than in past generations, and we have to work with this extended rhythm. A woman in her sixties may have another 30 years or more to live. If we accept in our minds that our lives are nearly over at retirement age, what do we do in the remaining one-third of our lives? Sit around the house?

Plan ahead. Develop areas of interest that can continue on throughout your life or begin new ventures. Keep lively and interested in the goings-on around you. The mind needs exercise as well as the body does. Have a youthful spirit that keeps your mind and body flexible.

The older we get, the more we understand the need to live fully in the present time. A younger person may postpone the things she wants to do or try thinking that there will always be time for it in the future. A woman in her fifties, or older, is more apt to seize the moment rather than let life's opportunities pass her by.

Contentment

Be content with what you have. So many people spend their whole lives thinking, "I'll be happy when...I have a new car, a bigger house, a better job, more money, the right partner, better health...." Decide to be happy and content *now*. Don't depend upon outer circumstances or you will always find something not quite right.

Laugh throughout Your Life

If we lose the ability to laugh, we lose the ability to enjoy life. Laughter is the magical type of medicine that heals all kinds of inner wounds and restores a radiant sense of well-being. Laughter heals the body and the mind and uplifts the soul. It is a great and powerful cure.

If the years slip by without the joyful murmurings of our spirit, the sparkle and zest for life slowly dwindles away until it is only a dim memory. Laughter not only uplifts our spirits to bring us courage to face the trials in life but also it brings joy in the moments of rest and helps unite the people of the world; when people can share in innocent laughter, they can see the common bond of humanity.

Your Highest Self

Rather than seeking only to oblige others, see all of your actions as a way to deepen your connection to a higher or greater consciousness. It will help you to remain in your own center of harmony.

When we live in the awareness of grace, then ennobling virtues grow within us. True grace is not limited to one component of life—physical, social, or spiritual. It integrates all three elements into one. Grace is a clear pathway that guides us throughout our entire lives.

Be a student of life. Discover your inner beauty and grace and encourage them to blossom and grow, untouched by the indignities of time. Let your life be filled with grace—and through your example, may you inspire others to seek the source of inner freedom and beauty that lies within themselves.

- There is an intrinsic beauty to every age.
- We are not our bodies, but our physical forms are the instruments that we use to express ourselves. Our "look" and comportment are the first clues that people have to our inner natures.
- Grace allows us to explore and develop the beauty of our spirits so they can shine forth and tell the world who we really are.
- Develop a personal style statement in harmony with your inner nature.

EPILOGUE

~

Make Your Body
a Storehouse of Energy

S cientists have proven that the entire universe is composed of energy that manifests in different forms. We can draw on this limitless supply to recharge our bodies.

There is a great exercise that can help rejuvenate the body and mind with fresh vitality and energy. It is simple to do once you become familiar with double breathing and the physical movements. It helps me whenever I feel fatigued or lethargic or when my mental vigor has diminished and been replaced with self-doubt and insecurity. The difference between feeling "on top of the world" or "down in the dumps" lies in our levels of energy.

This energization exercise is a fabulous way to start your day and can fit into any routine you may already have. The technique has three elements: a double breath, the physical movements, and concentration on drawing energy into the body. You will gain some benefit even if you only practice one aspect alone: double breathing, tensing and relaxing in waves of energy, or visualizing atoms of life force entering your body. But put all three together and you become a storehouse of energy!

I prefer practicing outside in the fresh air, although indoors is fine if you don't have a choice. To begin, you need to learn the double breath, which helps to draw more air into the lungs and to exhale it more completely. It can be performed while standing up or sitting down. I sometimes do a few cycles of double breathing while I'm sitting at the computer, just to liven up my brain.

Start by exhaling loudly through your mouth in a short, then longer and complete exhalation. Keep your throat relaxed to allow the air to flow unrestricted. You will hear a slight pause between the short and longer parts as you exhale. Then inhale through the nose in a short, then longer intake of breath. Again, you will feel a momentary hesitation between the short and longer parts of the inhalation as you completely fill your lungs with air. Keep your abdomen relaxed so you can use your diaphragm to inhale and exhale completely and with free-flowing enthusiasm. The purpose of the double breath is to wake up and rejuvenate the mind and your awareness and isn't as effective if done feebly. Repeat by exhaling all the air through your mouth using the double breath, then inhale using double breathing through the nostrils. Practice this a few times until you are comfortable with the technique and rhythm of it.

There should be a natural pause between your completed exhalations and inhalations, when your lungs are emptied and after being filled. This pause should be a relaxed part of the sequence, not an enforced holding in or out of air.

Next is the physical part of the exercise: Stand up and keep your posture upright, with your spine straight, shoulders slightly back, chin parallel to the floor, and arms down at your sides. Now raise your arms straight out to your sides at shoulder level so that your arms and body form a T. Exhale with the double breath while you bring your arms forward at shoulder height until your palms touch in front of you, still at shoulder level. With a double inhalation, start drawing your arms back to the original position out from your sides but with your hands fisted as you tense your whole body upward in a wave. Hold the tension in each body part as it rises through you.

Focus on this wave moving from your toes, feet, calves, knees, thighs, hips, and buttocks and through your abdomen and lower back, chest and upper back, shoulders and arms, and up to your neck, face, and head. Visualize the wave of tension as being vibrant with life-giving energy. When the wave reaches the top of your head, begin relaxing back down in reverse order, ending at your toes, as you exhale with the double breath and bring your arms back in front of you at shoulder level. You will finish with your palms touching straight ahead.

The wave of energy tension should flow quickly but smoothly up your body and then be released back down in a fluid motion: Inhale with energy tension rising up your body; double exhale as tension is relaxed back down. If you have an injured part of your body, use only a little tension there so the sore part isn't aggravated.

The physical movements along with the breath will take some practice in order for you to perform them as a fluid motion—but it only makes you feel better, so why not?

For the final step, in which you consciously draw on the life force that surrounds you as atoms of available energy, you will need to locate the medulla oblongata, the point through which you can visualize the life force entering your body. Feel at the base of your skull to locate the hollow place where the spine and skull meet. That is the area of the medulla oblongata.

Now, pull together all three aspects of the exercise.

1. Focus your attention on the area of the medulla oblongata. Start with your arms raised out to your sides and exhale with the double breath as you bring your palms together straight ahead. This gets you ready to begin the complete technique.

2. Then, as you begin your inhalation and wave of tension, visualize energy or healing light flooding into your body at the medulla oblongata to fill all your body's cells with new life as you tense each area. Envision and try to feel this vast source of re-

vitalizing atomic energy as it enters through the control point for the automatic systems of the body. Direct this flow with your thoughts to replenish your whole being. Concentrate deeply. Feel your body become magnetized with vitality.

3. After filling your body with this life force, begin your double exhalation and relaxation downward and feel the energy permeating every cell of your body. Do the exercise with your eyes closed, if you can, in order to deeply experience the benefits.

An inhalation and exhalation is one round of the exercise. Start your count on the first intake of breath. Your initial exhalation is mainly to prepare your lungs and body for a fresh supply of air. Practice three to six rounds whenever you want to fill yourself with radiant, life-affirming energy. We must possess energy in order to express it in our lives.

An alternate visualization technique can be practiced at times when you are unable to add the double breathing or physical movements. Focus upon healing light or energy flowing into your body when lying in bed or sitting in a chair. It will help you to feel connected to a broader source of energy other than the food you eat or the caffeine you may drink in coffee, tea, or sodas to keep yourself going.